WHEN BUILDINGS SPEAK

WHEN BUILDINGS SPEAK

Stories Told by Oregon's Historical Architecture

Interpreted and Illustrated

by Alice Cotton

ARTEMIS PUBLISHING

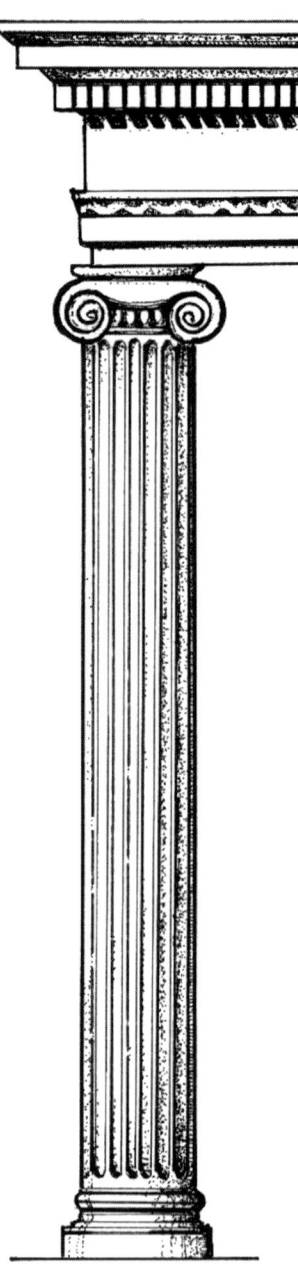
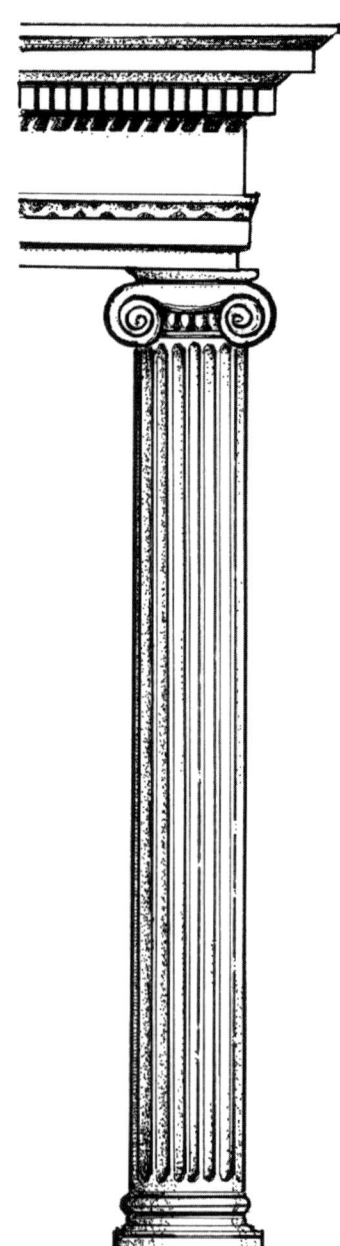

WHEN BUILDINGS SPEAK

Copyright © 2001 by Alice Cotton

All rights reserved. This book may not be reproduced in whole or in part in any form or by any means, electronic or mechanical, including photocopying, recording, or by any information storage and retrieval system now known or hereafter invented, without written permission from the publisher.

ISBN 0-9705542-0-6

Library of Congress Catalog Card Number:
00-110238

Cover and interior design by Dale Champlin
Illustration half-tone scanning by Jim Haegan of Revere Graphics
Edited by Alexandria Pallas-Weinbrecht
Printed by Publisher's Press
Back cover photo by Teresa Alexander

ARTEMIS
PUBLISHING

PO Box 16331
Portland, OR 97292-0331

Dedication

To my unbelievably supportive husband, David, and my
wonderfully intelligent, creative family who inspire me every day of my life.

Acknowledgements

My first "thank you" goes to my husband, *David Royer*, for his willingness to compromise his level of comfort in order for me to focus all of my energy on this book. I also thank him for patiently reading and viewing everything I showed him, for saying "Wow" a lot, and, when asked, for critiquing my art and carefully editing my writing. He kept me on track when I wavered and never let me abandon my dream.

My next set of acknowledgements goes to my immediate family and closest friends, who not only contributed their time and feedback as professionals, but are incredibly adept at making me feel like a million bucks.

Anna Filameno, my mother, screenplay writer, actress, for making me dig within myself to find my voice and let it out.

Alexandria Pallas-Weinbrecht, MA, my talented and brilliant sister, for editing my work and traveling with me to explore some of Oregon's treasures.

Christopher Henry Kaufman, DMA, my talented and brilliant brother, for his creative input and for encouraging me to be the artist I really am.

F. Wallace Kaufman, my father, organic farmer, house builder, political activist, who put the first paint brush in my hands.

John Weinbrecht, MBA, my brother-in-law, for being a most enthusiastic supporter and believer in my work and for his financial support for this project.

Jill Ostrow, my friend, author, visiting professor at Lewis and Clark College, for her unbelievably generous gift that helped to finance this project and for introducing me to the land of illustrating books through her own published works.

Aisha Munira, my friend, MST in Mathematics, for collaborating with me on our class called "Artistic Expressions of Mathematical Ideas," and for being a brilliantly visual mathematician.

Lisa Coffey, my friend, professional harpist, for helping me write my grant proposals and for her continuous support for my project.

Ken Lomax, my friend, musician, Oregon Historical Society Visitor Services/Recorded Sound Preservationist, for writing a letter of support for my grant request, for introducing me to the Oregon Historical Society, and for his financial support.

Jim Cameron, my friend, photographer, for helping me set up my camera and for turning me on to the Journal Building.

Byll Davis, musician and friend, for his financial support for this project.

Special thanks to:

The Northwest Reading Clinic, where I am a reading clinician every morning, for being flexible enough to give me the time off to create this book.

Lynn Kitigawa, medical illustrator, instructor at Pacific Northwest College of Art, for suggesting artistic improvements and for helping to keep me focused on maintaining high standards for my work.

William J. Hawkins III, FAIA, architect, author of *Classic Houses of Portland, Oregon: 1850–1950*, for his inspirational lecture on historical architecture and for the time he spent answering my questions and reviewing my work.

Virginia Miller, owner of the Barlow House, for giving up an afternoon to show me the house and tell me so many wonderful stories.

Mary Sauter, owner of the Palmer House, for taking the time in her busy day to tell me some good Palmer House stories.

Chief Jon Gagnon, Executive Petty Officer, and the *Tillamook Coast Guard*, for granting me free access to their picture albums and taking me on a tour of the newer Coast Guard facility and the historic guard house.

Oregon Historical Society library staff, who helped me locate information on many of these buildings and their interesting histories and for their work on renovating the Bybee House.

Joni Nelson, bookstore coordinator for Linn County Museum, for helping me correct the Moyer House text.

Nancy A. Niedernhofer and *Susan Halock*, National Register coordinators, State Historic Preservation Office, Oregon State Parks and Recreation Department, for helping me through the monumental task of compiling all the National Register documentation I needed, quickly and efficiently.

Historic Preservation League of Oregon, for offering lectures and activities that helped open my eyes to the wealth of beautiful and well-executed architecture in Oregon.

Mike McMenamin, owner of McMenamin's Pubs and Brewerys, *Liz Robbins*, general manager of Kennedy School McMenamin's, and *Tim Hills*, McMenamin's historian, for leaving their busy jobs to meet with me and go over the information on Kennedy Elementary School.

Richard Beer, director of programming and operations, Hollywood Theatre Project, for his input regarding the history of the Hollywood Theatre and for his exciting promotional ideas for my book.

Wallace Huntington, landscape architect, for allowing me to share this book with him and talk over one of our favorite subjects — historical architecture.

Bill Bachhuber, photographer, for doing such a wonderful job documenting my work.

Dale Champlin, graphic designer, for her artistic approach to graphic design and for making this book present so beautifully.

Bob Smith, "the book guy", for helping to make this book become a truely published work.

And I want to thank all the people and organizations not mentioned who gave their time and energy to provide information for the buildings in this book and for the other buildings I researched that didn't make it into this book.

Author's Note

All buildings included in this book are listed in the publication, *National Register Properties*, published by the Oregon State Historic Preservation Office.

Many of Oregon's historical buildings have been relocated, so I tried to include some of each building's original surroundings when possible.

I occasionally had to exercise "artistic license" by moving trees and shrubs in order to better view some of the buildings.

A glossary is included at the back of the book to help with unfamiliar architectural terms. In the glossary are inserts that are not found in the book itself, but are important for understanding architecture and its history.

The buildings are chronologically ordered according to the years when their styles appeared and not necessarily when they were actually built, although often the two coincide.

Contents

Opening			Page 13
No 1	The Bybee-Howell House	*Greek Revival*	Page 16
No 2	The Old Scotch Church	*Carpenter Gothic*	Page 18
No 3	The John M. Moyer House	*Italian Villa*	Page 20
No 4	The Jacob Kamm House	*Second Empire*	Page 22
No 5	The Sam Barlow House	*High Victorian Italian Bracketed*	Page 24
No 6	Union Station	*Richardsonian Romanesque*	Page 26
No 7	The Nathan Loeb House	*Queen Anne*	Page 28
No 8	The George Hochstedler House	*Stick*	Page 30
No 9	The James A. Flippin House	*Chateauesque*	Page 32
No 10	The John Palmer House	*Eastlake*	Page 34
No 11	The George F. Heusner House	*Shingle*	Page 36
No 12	The Journal Building	*Beaux Arts Classicism*	Page 38
No 13	Kennedy Elementary School	*Mediterranean*	Page 40
No 14	Hollywood Theatre	*Spanish Baroque*	Page 42
No 15	The Mark Ashley House	*Georgian Revival*	Page 44
No 16	The Haller-Black House	*Bungalow*	Page 46
No 17	Tillamook Bay Coast Guard Station	*Maritime Colonial*	Page 48
No 18	The Livesley House/Governor's Residence	*English Tudor Revival*	Page 50
No 19	The David T. Honeyman/Nan Wood House	*Colonial Revival*	Page 52
No 20	The George Pipes House	*Arts and Crafts*	Page 54
Closing			Page 56
Appendix			Page 57
Glossary			Page 64
Bibliography			Page 67
Index			Page 69

WHEN BUILDINGS SPEAK

"The story of home making ought to be as interesting as any other tale of adventure, of travels in a new land or even of love, for every home story is the best kind of a love story."

GUSTAV STICKLEY, *CRAFTSMAN BUNGALOWS*

Opening

As a young artist in New Orleans, I used to sit on a canvas stool with my pens and white drawing paper and illustrate as much Louisiana architecture as I could. The city was abundant with some of the most richly preserved and unique architecture in the country. I would take these drawings to Jackson Square, an artist's center in the middle of the French Quarter, and sell them to the many tourists who came by.

It was during this time in my life that I sat before a beautiful Mediterranean-styled house on Bourbon Street. The building was a marvel of detailed ironwork and stucco. Vines hung down from the orange tiles on the roof, and a stone pathway where someone had planted colorful flowers and exotic green plants led to an arched doorway. Carefully crafted ironwork furniture sat beside a trickling fountain where water fell from the gentle curves of the sculpture within it. It felt good to be there, and the drawing flowed easily into a work of art rather than simply into an outline of what the building looked like. I remember asking myself what it was about this building that was so deeply compelling? It would be many years before I found an answer to that question.

Later, as an illustrative artist and teacher in Portland, Oregon, I was preparing a lesson for a class called "Artistic Expressions of Mathematical Ideas" made up of continuing education students. My goal for the lesson was to focus on the mathematical concepts of volume, area, geometry, and the mathematical proportions of the golden rectangle used in early Greek and Roman architecture. I wanted to provide my students with an opportunity to plan and build architectural models of their own.

I believed the best way to accomplish this was to let the mathematical requirements of the class be driven by my students' desire to create something beautiful. In order to do this successfully, my students would need to see some examples of architecture that would fire their imaginations into total engagement.

Unfortunately, the classroom we worked in provided little inspiration, for it was simply a rectangular box with no windows and one door that was bordered with colorless plastic molding. The building that housed this room wasn't much better. It was purely a functional, pragmatic design, nothing more. I recalled that moment in New Orleans when a building became truly beautiful and inspirational to me. So I set out to find such an example in Oregon, one that would pique my student's creativity. I had no idea I was about to embark on an amazing journey.

An associate told me about a "Victorian" house that she had once visited. "I went there with my elementary school class and it was so beautiful and magical to me," she said. I was very interested in seeing the house she described until I found myself driving along a road lined with mundane looking gas stations, huge piles of dirt, a land supply company, used car lots, and shopping malls, wondering how anything of interest could possibly be found in such a setting.

The sun was beginning its late afternoon descent, and I was sure I would never find the building, when the landscape suddenly recessed into two lines of very tall black walnut trees. A small painted sign with the name of the house I was looking for had been placed in front of them.

I parked my car and walked across a long stretch of grass to where the line of trees ended. There I stood face-to-face with a house that looked like something right out of a fairy tale. It was a marvel of detail, adorned with a wealth of bracketed eaves and arched casement windows, towering bay windows, and a bayed portico entrance. I was deeply enchanted, so I grabbed my camera and photographed every corner and nook of this house. Once the film was developed, I felt compelled to draw it, as visions of my experience in New Orleans flooded back to me. This was my first encounter with Oregon's historical architecture.

This experience had a profound effect on me, and I wondered if, perhaps, there were more such buildings in Oregon. So, I began to collect resources from libraries, museums, book stores, and visitor centers to use as guides.

As I began to discover that there was, indeed, a wealth of outstanding historical architecture in Oregon, my original mission to find suitable buildings for my students evolved into the idea of creating a book — one that not only gave people a sense of the beauty of Oregon's architecture, but demonstrated their truly artistic qualities as well. I wanted to visit every building I found, but practicality forced me to narrow my sampling to the northwest quarter of the state where the majority of Oregon's historical architecture is located. My plan was to travel northwest from Portland to Astoria, south along the Oregon coast to Newport, then cross over to the Corvallis/Albany area, and come north along the Willamette River valley through Salem and back to Portland.

Once I started this journey through Oregon's historical architecture, it felt like a treasure hunt. I had great fun searching out buildings that were all but hidden within groves of Oregon firs and vine maple. Others were buried within remote, hard to find street sections of small towns. I found historical buildings residing beside beach paths, down commercial avenues, and along distant highways.

Everyone on my journey was kind and helpful. I never knew building owners or Chamber of Commerce, museum, and visitor center staff members had such a wealth of information. All of these people seemed as in love with their preserved historical architecture as I was becoming. With their help, I focused my survey on as many of the different architectural styles in Oregon as I could so as to showcase buildings constructed between the 1850s and 1940s.

During the course of researching and drawing these amazing buildings, I found myself drawn back to the question that arose in New Orleans. What was it about these buildings that was so deeply compelling to me? This issue was churning in my mind when I drove to see my last building. I went far into the region where the foothills of the Coastal Range level off to form a plains area. This flat plains area was sporadically highlighted with small farm houses and fields of freshly planted crops. After driving over a bridge that spanned a small creek, I found a wooden sign that signaled I had arrived. I parked my car and walked along a path that led through a thick grove of Douglas firs and cedar trees. At last I came to an open area where a small Gothic church stood amidst hundreds of old gravestones.

As I walked through this cemetery, I observed the engraved etchings — "Flora and Jacob," "Hawkins and Hanley," "mother," "son," "arrived in 1879," "our daughter died . . . aged 6." It became apparent to me that each gravestone was a tribute to a life, a time, and a people — an immigrant population that crossed an ocean and traveled across a great country to find a new home. I imagined the stories they could have told, the dreams they must have had that took them halfway around the world to build this church.

As I looked at the towering spire of the tiny Gothic church standing quietly within the cemetery, I realized that the building had housed over one hundred years of Sunday congregations, human prayers, human hopes, human fears, and sacred community rituals. I marveled at the steep vertical angles of its symmetry and woodwork. I was charmed by the pointed arches of its medieval windows and doorway. Inside, a handcrafted Celtic cross still hung in the sanctuary, preserved and revered to this day. I realized that I was getting closer to my answer. This little church not only represented an important architectural style with its own special charm and beauty, but it was a tribute — a monument to human events of the spirit and the heart.

What began as a quest to find architectural samples that would inspire my students' creativity had become a journey that richly satisfied my own artistic needs as well. By illustrating and researching these buildings, I found something wonderful and, in the end, felt the need to share it with you, my readers.

As you will find in the following pages, the buildings that I drew often spoke to me, and, with their guidance, I learned about the social attitudes, the materials and technologies, the economics, the aesthetic tastes, the hard work, and the creative vision of past human communities and individuals. They gave me the chance to explore geographical locations, native plant life, and the immigration patterns of the Northwest. I learned that there was a wonderful time in Oregon's history when a window of opportunity opened up for people to be innovative in creating a "new" Northwestern culture.

But, it wasn't until I began to look past the particular events heralding the turn of the twentieth century that I found the most intriguing aspect of all.

The buildings I had been studying and illustrating not only communicated the ideas of a people from one or two hundred years ago, but the ideas of people from one thousand years ago and beyond. For architecture, at its very core, represents the human response to one of our most basic needs — the need for shelter and how to best create it given the materials available. But once an understanding of the basic physics of gravity and the mechanics of structure were understood and developed, then, being the creatures that we are, we began creating and articulating ways in which to make these structures beautiful, mythical, metaphoric, and endearing.

With the help of these buildings, I had found a format in which to celebrate the importance, the vibrancy, and the passion that flows through the human heart when crafting a home, building a church, or designing a theater house. But the most amazing part of all was when I realized that, by pursuing my original question of "what was so compelling about these houses," I discovered that I had stumbled upon one of the most significant links to our earliest beginnings. I realized that every time I stood in front of and/or drew one of these buildings, I was being sent along a chain of human lives that stemmed back to the time when posts and beams were first applauded for the ingenious way they would hold up the mud, leaves, and sticks needed to keep one's head out of the rain. My journey through Oregon's architectural treasures led me to the undeniable conclusion that architecture is, at its essence, about who and what we are — beings bent on a solid and enduring survival, who are exceedingly clever, and who are at our best when embraced in the arms of our own creativity.

LOCATION: 13901 NW Howell Park Road, Sauvie Island, Oregon. Call 621-3344 or the Oregon Historical Society at 222-1741 for summer hours.

ARCHITECTURAL STYLE: Greek Revival, also called Classic Revival

BUILDER: James F. Bybee

DATE BUILT: 1856

OWNERS: James Bybee built this house in the Classic Revival style that was popular in the early and middle 1800s. He was a colonel and horse breeder from Kentucky who crossed the plains in a covered wagon to settle in Oregon with his wife, Julia. James Bybee was an early pioneer who, like others during the 1800s, made his fortune during the California "gold rush." He claimed 642 acres on Sauvie Island under the Donation Land Claim Act of 1850. This law gave each pioneer who settled in Oregon before December 1, 1851, 320 acres of land (a couple received 640 acres). After achieving financial success, Bybee became involved with his new Oregon community by being appointed one of the first Multnomah County Commissioners. He kept his love for horses alive by building several race tracks in the area.

After living in the house a few years, James Bybee sold it to a farming couple, Dr. Benjamin and Elizabeth Howell, and their three sons. Two of the Howell sons became prominent Northwest botanists, and one, Thomas, wrote a reference book called *Flora of Northwest America*. The third son became a distinguished farmer. When the Howells left in 1961, Multnomah County purchased seventy-five acres of the land for a park and game reserve.

Eventually, the Oregon Historical Society (OHS) purchased the house and carefully renovated it. The OHS paid special attention to keeping all renovations true to the house's historical integrity, and they planted gardens that contain a collection of native Oregon flora. It is now open to the public and is well worth a visit.

ANECDOTES: Greek Revival architecture originated in the temple architecture of ancient Greece, which was based on a post-and-lintel system of construction. The Bybee-Howell House has Tuscan-inspired columns with full cornice and entablature, a rectangular plan, symmetrically placed chimneys, fully pedimented gable ends, geometric volumes, and a symmetrical facade with a central entrance. During the first half of the 1800s, Americans embraced the formally organized concepts that originated in classical Greek art and architecture during the fourth and fifth centuries B.C. This resulted in a proliferation of early Greek architecture, sculpture, and furniture.

THE BYBEE-HOWELL HOUSE

It was morning, and the air smelled fresh and cool as I made my way towards a beautifully proportioned white sculpture called the Bybee-Howell House. It looked over the swamps and fields of Sauvie Island like a Greek goddess resting upon a high knoll. She was wrapped with the greens, yellows, and purples of Oregon grape, lilac, and ancient fruit trees. This goddess presented herself with the formal grace intended by the architects of ancient Greece. No wonder early pioneers gravitated to this architectural form. It must have given them a sense of order and peace within the untamed and rugged new land to which they had migrated. It is a proud structure, confident of its worldliness, and embraced within the golden proportions of nature itself. This goddess of Greek temple architecture demanded to be portrayed, so, of course, I drew her.

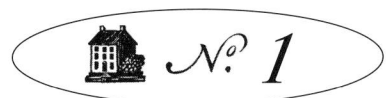

LOCATION: The Old Scotch Church is now known as the Tualatin Plains Presbyterian Church and is presently located on Old Scotch Church Road, north of Hillsboro, Oregon.

ARCHITECTURAL STYLE: Carpenter Gothic/Gothic Revival

BUILDERS: The twelve original congregational members who immigrated from Aberdeenshire, Scotland

DATE BUILT: 1876–78

OWNERS: The twelve original charter members of the Old Scotch Church were previously members of the "Free Church of Scotland." They settled in the Tualatin Plains area and decided to form a congregation. A couple named Jacob and Malinda Hoover donated the land so that the congregation could build a church. The church was built next to McCay Creek within a beautiful grove of evergreen trees. The Gothic style of architecture was most likely chosen for the church because it was similar to the congregation's home church in Scotland. The entire congregation volunteered labor and materials. A Celtic cross within the church sanctuary was handcrafted from a dogwood tree that had grown for many years at the home of church founders William and Margaret Chalmers.

In addition to the construction of the church, land was cleared and readied for a planned cemetery. Eight of the first twelve charter members, and many of their descendants, are presently at rest in the cemetery that surrounds the church.

The Reverend George Ross was the congregation's first pastor beginning in 1878. There have been twenty-six ministers who served the church over the years. The congregation has remained continuously active, and the church is still in use today.

ANECDOTES: Gothic architecture represented a major change that began in Europe as part of the romantic and picturesque movements of the late 1700s and early 1800s. These movements were spurred by the feeling that Classic/Greek Revival was too rigid, dull, and inhibited a style. The move towards Gothic Revival was a call for more interesting possibilities in the expression of symmetry, geometric volumes, and decorative potential.

Oregon's Gothic style of architecture appeared in the United States in conjunction with the availability of Andrew Jackson Downing's (1815–52) pattern books, such as *Cottage Residences*, *The Architecture of Country Houses*, which articulated the mood and spirit of the romantics. These books included plans, elevations, and details drawn by well-known architect Alexander Jackson Davis and made it possible for homeowners and local builders to do their own building. Gothic Revival long remained the most popular style for churches, especially during the 1860s to 1890s. Few examples remain in Oregon today, as many have been razed over the years.

THE OLD SCOTCH CHURCH

The sun was shining when I found this Gothic prize and its surrounding plethora of old gravestones nestled within a canopy of tall cedar and Douglas fir trees. As I walked towards the Old Scotch Church, I met Reverend Richard Zimmerman, the current pastor of the church, who invited me to explore the area after sharing some of the church's history with me. The scene was so picturesque and haunting, I wasn't surprised when I entered the cemetery and began to hear the voices of an immigrant culture trickling into my mind. Lovingly inscripted, old gray and brown gravestones were blanketed with the smell of roses that had been freshly placed in front of them. A mid-morning breeze brushed the sun's heat from my face as it must have done many years ago when these people labored long hard hours to erect this small Gothic church and cemetery. How better to memorialize that time when these people put forth such tremendous effort in making their dream come true than by drawing this scene, and sharing it with my readers.

Typical of Gothic architecture, the Old Scotch Church has a vertical thrust with its steeply pitched roofs, pointed arched windows, and high octagonal steeple. To further enhance the Gothic feeling, wood was placed in vertical and angular repetitive patterns using a board-and-batten outer wall covering. The church is of frame construction and has unique looking buttresses along the outer walls. A back section and basement have since been added.

20

LOCATION: 204 Main Street, Brownsville, Oregon

ARCHITECTURAL STYLE: Italian Villa

BUILDER: John M. Moyer built this house using materials processed in his own planing mill.

DATE BUILT: 1878–81

OWNERS: John M. Moyer was a carpenter by trade and an entrepreneur by nature. He came to Oregon from Ohio, was impressed with the Willamette valley, and decided to settle near the present-day town of Brownsville, which was co-founded by Hugh Leeper Brown and James Blakely. Like most entrepreneurs, Moyer tried many things that failed before, with the purchase of the Brownsville planing mill in 1863, he began to experience some financial success. He also helped organize the Eagle Woolen Mill in Brownsville in 1864, and, under Moyer's management, earnings generated by the mill increased each year. He eventually married the daughter of one of the co-founders of Brownsville.

It was during a period of growing prosperity from his local investments that Moyer built this Italian Villa. Moyer continued his efforts with businesses and banks until he died. He had extensive holdings in Linn County and had established a chain of stores in Portland. He is considered one of the stereotypical success stories of pioneers who came West, attained a high level of personal and economic success, and helped in the development of the area. John and Elizabeth Moyer owned this house until their deaths. The Hill Family Foundation of St. Paul, Minnesota, then acquired the house and donated it to the Linn County Historical Society. It is now a historical museum.

ANECDOTES: European Italian Villa buildings were made of masonry construction, so the Moyer House designers used flush wallboards of wood painted to simulate a stuccoed masonry surface. Like many Italian Villas, this house was designed in an asymmetrical style, with a low-pitched, hipped roof, wide eaves with decorative brackets, tall windows, a single door with a transom and sidelights, and an entranceway veranda. The Moyer House also has first-story, polygonal bay windows with pronounced moldings, delicate jigsaw-cut corner boards, a balustrade, and porch decorations.

The Moyer House was inspired by an Italian Villa featured in one of Andrew Jackson Downing's pattern books that had become very popular in the 1880s. Pattern books were written and illustrated by architects and included instructions for building popular styles of architecture. Andrew Downing and a group of other architectural entrepreneurs in both America and Great Britain began hosting a selection of popular styles in magazines and pattern books so that people could build on their own.

The Italian Villa was not only utilitarian and practical, but it was also meant to be an architecture that displayed wealth and good taste. This particular style eventually evolved into the Second Empire.

THE JOHN M. MOYER HOUSE

My sister, Alexandria, agreed to travel with me to see the Moyer House, but we seemed to be having a bit of trouble finding it. We were in a hurry, for the sun was beginning its late afternoon descent. I was feeling a bit frantic, as we had been driving for a long while past fields and barns, cows and sheep, desperately looking for a sign that said "Brownsville." Alexandria finally spotted one. "This way," she said as we rushed along the country roads. At last we entered the one block that comprised the town center of Brownsville, and it wasn't hard to spot what we believed to be the largest treasure box we had seen yet. Amid modest rural farms and town buildings, the Moyer House's jewel-like decorative features seemed to dance in front of our eyes. We parked and stood in front of it, pointing excitedly at what looked like diamonds and rubies and a roof lined with the spearheads and helmet tops of parading Roman soldiers.

LOCATION: 1425 SW 20th Avenue, Portland, Oregon

ARCHITECTURAL STYLE: Second Empire/French Second Empire with mansard roof construction

ARCHITECT: Justus Krumbein, born and trained in Germany

BUILDER: L. Therkelsen

DATE BUILT: 1871

OWNERS: Jacob Kamm, an immigrant from Switzerland, came to America with his parents. He was a high energy individual and held many jobs as a young man, including cabin boy and steamboat pilot. He also spent time as a student in marine technology. These experiences helped pave his way to an impressive career in the navigation business. He built the first Oregon stern-wheeler, the *Jennie Clark*, and became a principle stockholder in at least four river transportation companies and banks in the Northwest. Kamm was also involved in the building of Astoria, where he was a bank president and land owner. When he died, he was a wealthy man with his own block of buildings in Portland and an estate outside of town. The Kamm House was Portland's first mansion.

The Kamm House became a children's museum when Kamm moved out in the early 1900s. The house was moved from its original location, where Lincoln High School is now located, in 1951. It was restored by Eric Ladd, who envisioned the house as part of his "Old Colony" project of antique houses in Portland, which included the Lincoln House (a 1905 Lewis and Clark Exposition model), the Miller House, St. Mary's Chapel, and the Glisan Building.

Ladd sold the house to Peter Hoffman. Hoffman had the house scheduled for demolition in order to build a large commercial structure. However, due to financial problems, Hoffman decided to sell the house, which at that time had become abandoned and derelict. Finally, the house was placed into safe hands when it was sold to Ron Emerson and William Hawkins, who formed Kamm House Partnership, an architectural and property development firm. They restored the Kamm House to its present form.

ANECDOTES: This architectural style is represented with an asymmetrical shape and dormer windows in a mansard roof. It has wide decorative quoins and tall segmentally arched windows. It has a belt cornice that divides the stories of the house and smoothly fitted wood siding to simulate a smooth masonry look. Groups of three or four windows are in polygonal bays and are surrounded with corniced window trim. In the front, there are paired doors with a transom and a small vestibule inside.

When Eric Ladd bought the Kamm House for his "Old Colony" project, he turned it into a restaurant. The restaurant eventually folded and funding for the project began to dry up. The Kamm House was scheduled for demolition, and Ladd spent an enormous amount of energy trying to save it. Finally

THE JACOB KAMM HOUSE

When I first saw the Kamm House, I was awed by the originality of its design and the elegance of its stature. It currently sits on the slope of a hill overlooking Portland. It is not ostentatious, yet it is beautiful and retains an aura of royalty. This is a building of many crowns. Its windows are crowned with arched cornices and large keystones. Its entrance door boasts an arched portico that proudly wears a pronounced set of urns. The front bay window is adorned with a handsome balustrade, and the Kamm House's projected face is crowned with scalloped shingles. Atop its entirety, we find its most prized crown of all: its rare mansard roof.

The Kamm House has been moved from its original location where it was surrounded by fruit trees, an ancient black walnut tree, a magnolia tree, and a cherry tree. I wanted some of the flora from its original site to be represented, so I included a few of them in the fore- and background.

in 1959, the house was declared one of the "ten most significant designs of a century of Oregon architecture" by a statehood centennial committee. The Kamm House was put on the National Register in 1974.

Mansard roof styles (straight sloped roofs) were presented in pattern books such as Henry Hudson Holly's *Country Seats* and A. J. Bicknell's *Specimen Book of One Hundred Architectural Designs*. Mansard roofs became popular for a time.

Second Empire style was born in France and quickly became a favorite of the burgeoning upper middle class in Europe and America. It is not a revival style, but it was a contemporary architectural movement that offered a more sophisticated look.

LOCATION: 24670 South Highway 99E, Canby, Oregon

ARCHITECTURAL STYLE: High Victorian Italian Bracketed, also referred to as Italianate

BUILDER: William Barlow built this house. It is believed a master carpenter named Mr. Kidd was hired by Barlow to supervise its construction.

DATE BUILT: 1885

OWNERS: William Barlow and his family were the first owners. When William died in 1904, his oldest daughter, Mary, sold the house to Samuel Berg and his family. After two generations and forty-five years later, the Bergs sold the Barlow House to an elderly couple, Mr. and Mrs. Henry Page. After twenty-one years, in the 1970s, the Barlow House was up for sale again when a woman named Virginia Miller fell in love with it and purchased it in 1973. Miller was committed to restoring the property to its original form and placed the house on the National Register.

ANECDOTES: William's father, Samuel Barlow, was an important historical figure who was instrumental in developing early transportation routes to aid emigrants coming to Oregon. Sam Barlow and his wife, Susanna, traveled with the largest wagon train to come to Oregon (1000 wagons, 5000 people). Sam decided he needed a more direct route to make his Donation Land claim (see Donation Land Claim Act of 1850) in the Oregon City area. So, with the help of his three sons, he constructed Barlow Road, which stretched from The Dalles to Oregon City, Oregon, in 1845. Barlow Road was the first overland route through the Cascade Mountain range.

In 1852, the Barlow sons bought their father's land when Sam moved to Canemah (an Indian word meaning "the place of the canoes") to entrepreneur a river steamboat company. William Barlow was influential in developing the small community of Barlow, where William owned a sawmill and the Barlow Bank and Land Development Company. William's second wife, Sarah, was from a wealthy southern family in Virginia, and she influenced William to construct the first Barlow mansion in the style of a southern plantation. Unfortunately, this house was destroyed by a fire, and William built the next Barlow mansion in the Italianate style we see today. Sarah's influence stretched a bit farther when she convinced William to send for the walnuts that were planted in two lines leading to the mansion's front doors. These were the first black walnut trees in Oregon.

During the 1880s in Portland, which by that time had become a bustling commercial center, hundreds of houses were constructed in the Italianate style. Apparently, the population grew tired of the Greek Revival and Gothic styles that had once proliferated in Oregon cities and towns. The Italianate style provided a nice blending of elegance and free expression with its classic and decorative features.

Like other Italianate buildings of the time, the Barlow House is symmetrical (although many Italianate homes were asymmetrical as well). Typical Oregon

THE SAM BARLOW HOUSE

The Barlow House represents my first experience with historical Oregon architecture. An associate told me she had visited this building as a child and that it was certainly worth a visit. I found the Barlow mansion at the end of a row of tall black walnut trees. It rested elegantly within a background of white clouds and turquoise sky. There it sat, smiling proudly at all who walked by, as it bathed in the golden rays of the setting sun. It looked as though no one was home, so I walked around the front of the house taking photographs of window cornices, stairway balusters, roof brackets, even the Victorian lamps that I could see inside the windows. Suddenly a woman came walking towards me. I explained what I was doing, and the woman seemed unperturbed, for apparently she was used to artists and photographers lurking about her property. We chatted a bit before she proceeded to take her evening walk. Later, I discovered that I had met Virginia Miller, the woman responsible for saving and restoring this old mansion from its demise in the 1970s.

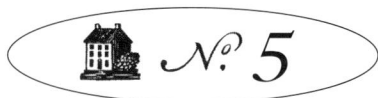

Italianate houses were based on the rectangular-shaped Italian palazzo (palace) with the addition of bay windows. The Barlow House is decorated with window cornices, paneled frieze works supported by oversized brackets, entablature heads over the remaining windows, a low-pitched, hipped roof, projecting eaves with decorative brackets, paired doors and transom, and a single bay entrance. The all-cedar house is a balloon frame construction.

LOCATION: 800 SW 6th Avenue, Portland, Oregon

ARCHITECTURAL STYLE: A variation of Richardsonian Romanesque Revival

DATE BUILT: 1892–96

ARCHITECTS: The Van Brunt and Howe architectural firm. Henry Van Brunt trained under British-born architect George Snell, who had an important practice in Van Brunt's hometown of Boston. Van Brunt also apprenticed in New York with Richard M. Hunt, the first American architect to be trained at the Ecole des Beaux Arts in Paris. Van Brunt helped to collaborate on the designing of Union Passenger Station in Massachusetts, which integrated the massing of stone-faced, diverse forms with a 212-foot tower, much like the one used on Portland's Union Station.

Frank Maynard Howe, also from Massachusetts, was a student in the very first class of the newly formed architectural program at MIT. He apprenticed in Van Brunt's firm and eventually became Van Brunt's partner. They moved to Kansas City, where they established themselves as a leading architectural firm.

OWNERS: Henry Villard, a German financier, bought a twenty-two block "frog pond" called Couch Lake on which he wished to build "The Grand Union Depot" using the reputable New York architectural firm of McKim, Mead, and White. He envisioned the depot to be a terminal station that would house all the major railroads he had purchased and owned in the late 1880s. However, in 1893, Henry found himself in financial difficulty, and the depot project had to be abandoned.

The Portland Development Commission eventually purchased the station and hired architects Van Brunt and Howe to complete its design and construction. The new terminal, Union Station, opened its doors in 1896. Amtrak bought Union Station from the city of Portland and still runs trains through the station today. The City of Portland now owns Union Station once again and, as the writing of this book, is planning to renovate it.

ANECDOTES: The Romanesque features of this building include its massive tiled roofs, fine grillwork, and tall towers. Its one-hundred-fifty-foot tower is topped with a four-sided clock. The clock, designed by Seth Thomas, was installed in 1895. In the 1880s, Portland, where all the western railroads met, became the economic center of Oregon, and Union Station became the leading Oregon railroad terminal. The railroads that fed into Union Station facilitated immigration into Oregon from all regions of the country. Union Station remains the oldest major passenger terminal on the West Coast.

Architect Henry Richardson initiated the Romanesque Revival movement, which was an offshoot of the Gothic Revival style on the east coast. The Romanesque style employed massive forms of solid masonry, steeply pitched triangular gables, rounded turrets, polygonal bays, stone walls, and facade dormers. A monograph of Richardson's work was published soon after his death in 1886, which had a major influence throughout the country. The Richardsonian Romanesque style was rooted in the medieval Romanesque architecture of France and Spain.

UNION STATION

I love trains, and I love train stations. So it was fortunate for me that Portland raised the status of Union Station to that of a national historical landmark. The building speaks to you. Look up above its tall clock tower and you will see its timeless message, "Go By Train," which many people did and still do. The station stands as a testament to the rapid growth of Oregon, particularly Portland, at the turn of the century—a time when people from Europe and all regions of the United States came looking for new opportunities, new beginnings, and new homes. They were adventurers, merchants, builders, farmers, railroad workers, entrepreneurs, and gold diggers. They crowded through the train station gates smelling of travel wear and perfume. They wore formal suits, work clothes, or their native cultural attire. They were frightened, excited, tired, and determined, and they kept arriving until Oregon grew into the distinctive state it has now become. Union Station is very large, so I focused on drawing only one portion of the building—its main entrance with the wraparound arcaded veranda and tall clock tower.

28

LOCATION: 726 NW 22nd Avenue, Portland, Oregon

ARCHITECTURAL STYLE: Queen Anne

BUILDER: Rudolph Becker

DATE BUILT: 1893

OWNERS: Rudolph Becker built this house in what was considered a fashionable residential area called King's Second Addition. The King's Second Addition encompassed some of the largest and finest Victorian houses of the late 1800s. Unfortunately, Becker and his family never lived in this exquisite house. It is believed Becker fell victim to the 1893 Panic (an economic depression in Oregon), and like many others during that time, Becker was forced to lease his house. Luckily for him, Nathan Loeb and his family became Becker's tenants until Loeb's death in 1905.

Nathan Loeb was born in Germany and came to America with his two brothers to operate a clothing business in California. Later, they opened a merchandising business in Oregon. Nathan Loeb became quite prosperous and active in the Portland Jewish community. He was a founding member of the Temple Beth Israel congregation, and he and many of his descendants became prominent business professionals in the Portland area. The house was later owned by Dr. and Mrs. Jack B. Blumberg. At present, it has been broken up into several apartments and is, as of the writing of this book, on sale.

ANECDOTES: The Queen Anne architectural style is the epitome of what we now call "Victorian period" architecture, acquiring its name during the reign of Queen Victoria (1840–1901) and is characterized by picturesque architectural forms inspired by medieval buildings. In the 1880s, new fortunes were being made in Oregon, and new tastes had evolved from the more "conservative" Italianate styles to the more inventive and original form of the Queen Anne.

The Queen Anne architectural style was identified with the Scottish-born architect Richard Norman Shaw, whose domestic work in England was extremely eclectic. Shaw pulled ideas from a range of sources, including Classical, Tudor, and Flemish architecture, featuring steeply pitched roofs, asymmetrical designs, shaped gables, sash windows, tall chimneys, and highly decorative compositions.

Queen Anne houses represented a move towards an architecture that could accommodate a variety of individual needs and tastes. Home builders had an abundance of charming features to choose from that were quite diverse in style. Queen Annes were featured in pattern books as well, which helped to popularize the style. This architecture seemed the perfect vehicle for expressing the individuality of homeowners and architects, as well as for displaying one's wealth.

THE NATHAN LOEB HOUSE

Seemingly random, the facade of this Queen Anne is actually a skillfully arranged collage of variegated shapes and textures that translate into a dynamic work of art. You can linger about the face of this building, as I did to behold the arched palladian window with its delicately colored stained-glassed windows. Then you can follow along the palladian's bayed sides into the recesses of the porch where a curious porch light hovers over a balustraded stairway. Intricate stained-glass designs welcome you at the paired entranceway doors and transom. Another ornately stained-glass design parallels the doors inside a pedimented window. Your gaze can now wander up the classical columns to the second level porch where two more stained-glass designs decorate a round window and an upstairs single door behind a full length balustrade. Then take a look up past the lines of classical cornices and dentils, over the sawn scrollwork on the upper tympanum, until you reach the Nathan Loeb House's steeply pitched roof. Ah, yet another window style, and still another as your gaze shifts to the right where there is more decorative wood siding, more scrollwork. And finally your eyes will come to rest on a beautifully crafted sunburst pattern surrounding the largest window of all. Yes, Mr. Becker, you definitely have our attention.

LOCATION: 237 6th Street SE, Albany, Oregon (in the historic Hackleman District)

ARCHITECTURAL STYLE: Stick

BUILDER: George Hochstedler

DATE BUILT: 1889

OWNERS: In the 1880s, George Hochstedler owned the Hochstedler and Sears Planing Mill in Albany, Oregon. Hochstedler and his partner, architect Ed Zeiss, supplied plans and instructions for builders. Hochstedler had his home constructed using the finest wood products manufactured by the mill. Later, Hochstedler became the Albany branch manager of Sugarpine Door and Lumber Company. The Hochstedler House was eventually sold to general store owner Charles Parker, whose wife Hadie was a music teacher in Albany. As of the writing of this book the Hochstedler House was being used as a triplex apartment building.

ANECDOTES: Stick style architecture was considered one of the first truly American forms, where wood was seen as a medium in its own right rather than as a substitute for stone and masonry. (Many of the buildings you have seen thus far used flush wood siding to mimic stucco or masonry.) What better place for this style to proliferate than in the Northwest where wood was so abundant. Wood pieces were placed in vertical, horizontal, and diagonal angles over the siding at places where the unseen structure frame could be "seen" or accented. Stick work was used on Queen-Anne- and-Eastlake-styled buildings for its decorative value. The Hochstedler House has a steeply pitched, hipped roof combined with gabled roofs on all elevations.

Gervase Wheeler's *Rural Homes*, written in 1851, featured the Stick-styled house, which helped to popularize this style throughout the United States. The Stick style allowed for creative interpretation since it had no historical precedent. Local carpenters and builders who knew little about historical architecture could try out their own ideas, many of which were strikingly handsome.

The Hochstedler House is located in what is called the Hackleman's Second Addition to Albany, Oregon. The Hackleman District was named after Abner Hackleman, a farmer from Iowa who, in 1845, immigrated to Oregon. He crossed the plains with oxen teams, took up a claim under the Donation Land Claim Act of 1850, and settled in the area.

Some of Albany's (and much of Oregon's) population began to arrive when the "Oregon Fever" broke out in 1840 in response to the California gold rush. The men, mostly farmers, went south to find gold and left the old men, women, and children behind to mind the farms. When they returned home, they had nuggets and gold dust. The value of this gold provided enough wealth to finance the construction of new cities and industries in Oregon.

Between 1850 and 1855, the possibilitites of claiming free land through the Donation Land Claim Act brought in trains of covered wagons from the

THE GEORGE HOCHSTEDLER HOUSE

I found this quaint Stick-styled house residing deep within the Willamette valley in Albany, Oregon. Being a lover of natural wood, I was immediately intrigued with the wood design that makes up the siding. The diagonal, vertical, horizontal, and radiating wood panels seem to parallel the house's inner structure, which would suggest that the house's wood frame was regarded as a valued component of the design aesthetic. What a delightful idea. The Stick style creates a rustic, yet subtle facade so, in order not to distract my viewers from its unique wood patterns, I stayed away from incorporating an embellished background in this picture. It seems the designers of the Hochstedler House felt the same way, for, with the addition of decorative verge boards, brackets, balusters, and scroll siding, the viewer is not distracted from the Hochstedler House's unique Stick design.

eastern United States. Small Oregon towns began to grow as people gathered together to build communities, towns, and economic networks.

Because of its location along the Willamette River valley, the city of Albany benefited as transportation technology improved and expanded. Steamboats brought necessities and provided new trading and sales opportunities. Albany became a stopover point for the California Stage Company, the first major stage in the west. In 1871, the first locomotive came through Albany. Albany grew and prospered at a steady pace, becoming a major manufacturing and transportation hub of the Willamette River valley.

32

LOCATION: 620 Tichenor, Clatskanie, Oregon

ARCHITECTURAL STYLE: Chateauesque/French Renaissance

BUILDERS: Markwell and Sons of San Andreas, California

DATE BUILT: 1900

OWNERS: "A man's home is his castle, and so I built mine to look like one," said James A. Flippin. He built this house for his son, Thomas Flippin, who resided there until Thomas and his wife, Florence Elliott, separated and the house was sold.

James Flippin was the progenitor of the Flippin family in Oregon. Originally from Tennessee, he was a member of the Applegate overland party that pioneered the Southern Immigrant Route in 1845. At nineteen, James Flippin decided to pan for gold in California. He happened to be at Sutter's Mill when gold was discovered and panned himself a small fortune. He went back home to Tennessee, got married, and made his way to Oregon. James's son, Thomas Flippin, began his career as a "skid greaser" on a "bull team" and proceeded to work his way up to become the owner of a sawmill. The Flippins represent, like several other families in this book, the stereotypical "pioneer comes to the Northwest and makes fortune" story of the 1800s.

Another one of James's sons, Will Flippin, had a major role in making the hand-hewn shingles for the roof and siding. Apparently, an enormous amount of work and artistry went into the creation of the Flippin House's shingle siding.

The property was acquired in 1959 by the Columbia County Council of Senior Citizens, Inc.

ANECDOTES: The Flippin House is currently operated as a partial historical house museum, with senior citizen volunteers serving as guides. It is also the town's senior center. Meals are served at noon, and the center offers "meals on wheels" and transportation for its growing elderly population, which, as of the writing of this book, numbers over one thousand. The people in Clatskanie call this house "The Castle."

The Flippin House has two round towers, a steep gabled roof, fish scale shingles, and a classical porch, all of which were indicative of the French Renaissance architectural style. The Flippin House was the grandest residence in the small logging and farming community of Clatskanie. Its symmetrically organized structure has a Colonial Revival porch entry with Tuscan columns and an upper deck railing of balusters. This "castle" contains fourteen rooms and two fireplaces. At one time, the upstairs rooms were used as boarding rooms. The rooms are large, and several have their own bathrooms.

THE JAMES A. FLIPPIN HOUSE

When my sister and I left Portland to look for houses along the Oregon coast, the Flippin house was the first example of historical architecture we saw. It was a glorious sight, sitting high on a hill overlooking the small Oregon town of Clatskanie. We walked around the entire building in awe of the intricate shingle work on all sides. On one side, there were colored shingles that depicted a scene of a man walking on the moon, replete with a star and a comet. On another side, we saw colored shingles that were placed in rows of diamond-shaped polygons. Even the foundation stonework was hand-etched with various patterns. While exploring the house, we were lucky enough to meet Marge Tuomi, the senior advocate for the Flippin House senior center. She talked to us about the senior center organization that now runs the senior center and the Flippin House museum. We were very impressed with the work of this organization, for they provide transportation services, meals, and recreation for the area's elderly citizens. We were also impressed with the splendor and the location of the Flippin House. It was peaceful and beautiful: an Oregon treasure in the form of a "castle" overlooking the town and the hills beyond.

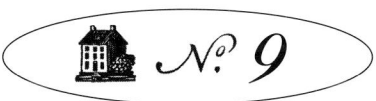

LOCATION: 4314 North Mississippi Avenue, Portland, Oregon

ARCHITECTURAL STYLE: Eastlake/Queen Anne

BUILDER: John Palmer, a builder/contractor by trade, built this house.

DATE BUILT: 1890

OWNERS: Original owner, John Palmer, only lived in this house for a few years. After his wife died, he sold the house, at which time the Palmer House changed ownership a number of times before it landed in the hands of musicians Oskar and Lotta Hoch. The building housed not only the Hochs, but it also housed the Multnomah Conservatory of Music from 1910 until 1935. The conservatory held classes in violin, piano, trumpet, and music theory. Later, before it was sold, Mrs. Hoch would sit in the window and look out for long periods of time, causing rumors throughout the neighborhood about witches and hauntings.

In 1968, the Palmer House was bought and renovated by Mary and Richard Sauter. The Sauters had to do some extensive clean up and repair work. Various occurrences in the Palmer House led the Sauters to believe the house was haunted. "We've had [a ghost] on and off since we moved here," says Mary Sauter. Mary believes it is Lotta Hoch. "She has a very strong presence in the house." At one point, there was talk of the house being haunted when one end of the Sauter's carpets began to move around. In time, they found the real cause; "a facia board was missing under the porch and the wind would blow under there," says Mary.

The Sauters took great care in restoring the house to its historical Victorian roots. At one point, the house required thirty-four different types of wallpaper in four adjoining rooms. Bruce Bradbury, owner of a wallpaper company, took on the job and gave the Sauters a break in the cost. In 1985, the city of Portland awarded the Sauters the first residential Preservation Award ever given for their excellence and effort in their renovation of the Palmer House. This is an award that unfortunately is not given anymore.

Mary Sauter says that since the Sauters had the house, it has been filled with love. During the thirty-two years that they have been there, they raised their children, made it into a bed and breakfast, and have shown it to the public.

The Palmer House is currently up for sale, and Mary Sauter hopes that whoever buys it will love it as much as the Sauters have and that they would try very hard to continue restoring it in an authentic fashion.

ANECDOTES: In America and in Europe, the Victorian era was characterized by prosperity, self-confidence, and extravagance. The success of industrialization had created an optimistic class of the newly rich ready to flaunt its wealth. Advances in technology made it possible for homeowners and builders to construct fashionable residences. It is interesting to note that Charles Locke Easklake, whose name is ascribed to this style, disassociated himself from the "Eastlake style" as it developed. For some reason, a myth began that stated that this type of ornamentation

THE JOHN PALMER HOUSE

Driving along a hill within a modest north Portland neighborhood, I came upon this festival of ornamentation. Gables, bays, doorways, and windows were placed in sections like movements in a symphony. Each section was composed of its own set of notes, or in this case, its own set of ornamental features; yet they seemed to work together to create this unique composition called the Palmer House. Whether the outcome is cacophonous or harmonious remains subjective and debatable. The haunting episode of the Sauters added yet another dimension to this multilayered creation; for at a moment in time, the Palmer House had become the proverbial "haunted house" of the neighborhood. Even now, as it is changing hands once again, it sits empty, almost foreboding, like a witch's castle on Halloween.

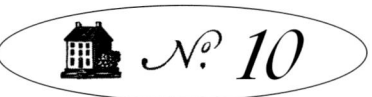

was his innovation. But it wasn't. He actually thought that these "Eastlake" buildings were quite overdone and bizarre.

Eastlake buildings are some of the most dramatic and extreme statements in the history of American architecture. It is difficult to draw precise lines between the Queen Anne and the Eastlake styles, for their basic plans are almost identical. "Eastlake" is a term that more correctly describes a style of ornamentation rather than a building structure. The Eastlake ornamental additions on Queen Anne houses make them appear very rhythmic and whimsical in composition — a fitting style for a building that has housed musicians for many years.

The restoration of this building had a profoundly positive effect in that, during a time of social unrest, it encouraged the surrounding community homeowners to restore their own homes and work towards the rehabilitation and maintenance of their community.

LOCATION: 333 NW 20th Avenue, Portland, Oregon

ARCHITECTURAL STYLE: Shingle

DATE BUILT: 1894

ARCHITECT: Architect Edgar Max Lazarus was part of a wave of architects who came to Portland at the turn of the century. He established himself in the Portland architectural scene, producing houses of first-rate quality. Edgar Lazarus was a member of the architectural firm of Lazarus, Whitehouse, and Fouilhoux in the 1880s. He designed many notable buildings in and around Portland, including the Portland Art Museum, the Vista House on Crown Point, the U.S. Customs House, and many others. In the 1880s, numerous architectural publications that featured the Shingle style attracted Lazarus, and he used Shingle architectural ideas for many of his Portland residences.

OWNERS: The first owner was a man named E. D. McKee. In 1905 through 1907, Henry W. Goode, a utilities executive and president of the Lewis and Clark World's Fair, lived in the house. Later, George Heusner and his family rented the house in 1907. The house was not correctly named, but George Heusner's reputation as an ambitious realtor who was responsible for the development of several residential areas in north and northeast Portland may have overshadowed the first owners of the building. He was also a clerk in the U.S. District Court. In the 1920s, the Heusner House was a boarding house and home for young ladies. Rooms were provided for "well bred and well supervised young women." More recently, it has been divided into apartments.

ANECDOTES: Shingle-style architecture became vogue for a period of time at the turn of the century. Its sweeping roofs, old world towers, and the tall stone chimneys were said to give a feeling of romanticism. Shingle-styled houses used simple geometric forms, with shingles covering the upper stories and triangular gables. The rest of the house was usually covered with stone and shingles, as with the Heusner House. The architectural design is asymmetrical, and like its sister designs — the Queen Anne, Eastlake, and Stick styles — it became quite popular.

With this particular house, architect Edgar Max Lazarus experimented with a variety of new window treatments, such as the addition of the eyebrow dormer near the top, the partially recessed dormer with a hipped roof, and the various groupings of windows around the house. To give the house a slightly medieval look, the window top sashes at the second floor have diagonal mullions, while the bottom sashes have a single pane. Most of Lazarus's houses had widely projecting eaves and graceful concave curves at the eave extensions. Notice the steeply pitched gable extending from the front and the extensive wraparound veranda complete with stone piers and railings. The three massive chimneys represent another prominent romantic feature of the Shingle-styled house. Lazarus used ashlar-patterned sandstone for the stonework.

THE GEORGE F. HEUSNER HOUSE

The graceful sweeping shapes, the bell tower, the extended eaves gliding from a steeply pitched roof, and the combination of wood shingles and massive stone gave me the feeling that I had awakened into a romantic, picturesque world where the flowers could talk and wood elves were ready to gather around me. I would most certainly be escorted to see the Wood Princess who dwells within, where we would sip some tea and discuss the most current deeds of the adventurous and magical. To draw such a house is to still the moment, to breathe in the mood fully. Drawing is the best way I know to capture such a compelling image, and the pleasantest way I know to remember a few of my favorite hobbit tales.

Nº 11

38

LOCATION: 806 SW Broadway, Portland, Oregon

ARCHITECTURAL STYLE: Beaux Arts Classicism

ARCHITECTS: The Reid Brothers (James William and Merrit J.), a San Francisco-based firm, which specialized in the field of newspaper plant designs. The Reid brothers were born in Canada.

DATE BUILT: 1912

OWNERS: The Journal Building (also known as Jackson Tower) was erected to become the headquarters of a Portland newspaper called the *Oregon Journal*. Under the leadership of publisher C. S. Jackson, who acquired the newspaper in 1902, the *Oregon Journal* became one of Portland's major newspapers. Jackson's policy for the newspaper was to be fearless and independent. The other major newspapers at that time were the *Oregonian* and the *Telegram*. Jackson's paper carried on into the 1980s, with presses rolling out over 72,000 newspapers an hour. In 1958, the building was sold to Theodore Bruno. In 1970, the building was sold to B & D Development, a privately owned company, who upgraded the building and reactivated its perimeter of lights that had been dark for many years. It is now used as an office building.

ANECDOTES: The Journal Building, a twelve-story steel-framed skyscraper, features a "wedding cake" design topped with a dramatic clock tower. The building is one hundred feet square at the base, the area of a quarter of a city block. At the entrance level, there are three colossal Roman-arched openings with recessed baroque framing elements. Beneath the entire structure is a two-story basement that once accommodated the press room of the *Oregon Journal*.

One of the striking attributes of the Journal Building is the fact that the architects used glazed terra cotta as the exterior sheathing material over the building's steel frame. This terra-cotta glaze kept the building fireproof and contributed to its sculptural aspects.

The type of terra cotta used on the Journal Building was made of hard-baked, fine-grained clay. It was similar to brick, but made of a finer grade of clay and fired at a higher temperature. Generally, terra cotta was manufactured in hollow blocks 4 inches deep with faces typically 12 x 18 inches. The terra-cotta firms of the time employed sculptors to make plaster and clay models for the ornamentation. The dominant firm manufacturing handmade architectural terra cotta for Portland was Gladdin, McBean, and Company of San Francisco.

Following a trend that began with the 1905 Lewis and Clark Exposition, the outline of the Journal Building was illuminated with a series of lights. During World War II, the building lights were shut down to conserve energy. Then in the 1970s,

THE JOURNAL BUILDING

A photographer friend of mine told me that the building at the southwest corner of Salmon and Sixth Avenue was being razed to make room for a new downtown commercial building project. This just happened to provide me with the rare opportunity to see the Journal Building in full view. I was immediately there with my camera, sneaking past the demolition squad's wire fencing one full block away from the Journal Building. I could see all twelve stories of the Journal Building unhindered by anything save a few white flakes of demolished cement dust from the razed building. The Journal Building looked handsome with its large clock embedded in the terra cotta of its classical Beaux Arts detailing. The building actually looked a bit overdressed amid the taller and exceedingly less ornate modern buildings surrounding it — a classical traditionalist wearing a formal tuxedo while everyone else was wearing their everyday business grays.

№ 12

the Journal Building's newest owners, B & D Development, turned all eighteen hundred lights back on.

Beaux Arts architecture refers to the American Renaissance period from about 1885 to the 1920s and includes the Italian Renaissance, Neoclassical Revival, and French baroque architectural styles. In America, these buildings featured facades of pristine white limestone, buff color, or yellow brick in a narrow gauge, often accented with sculptural ornamentation.

40

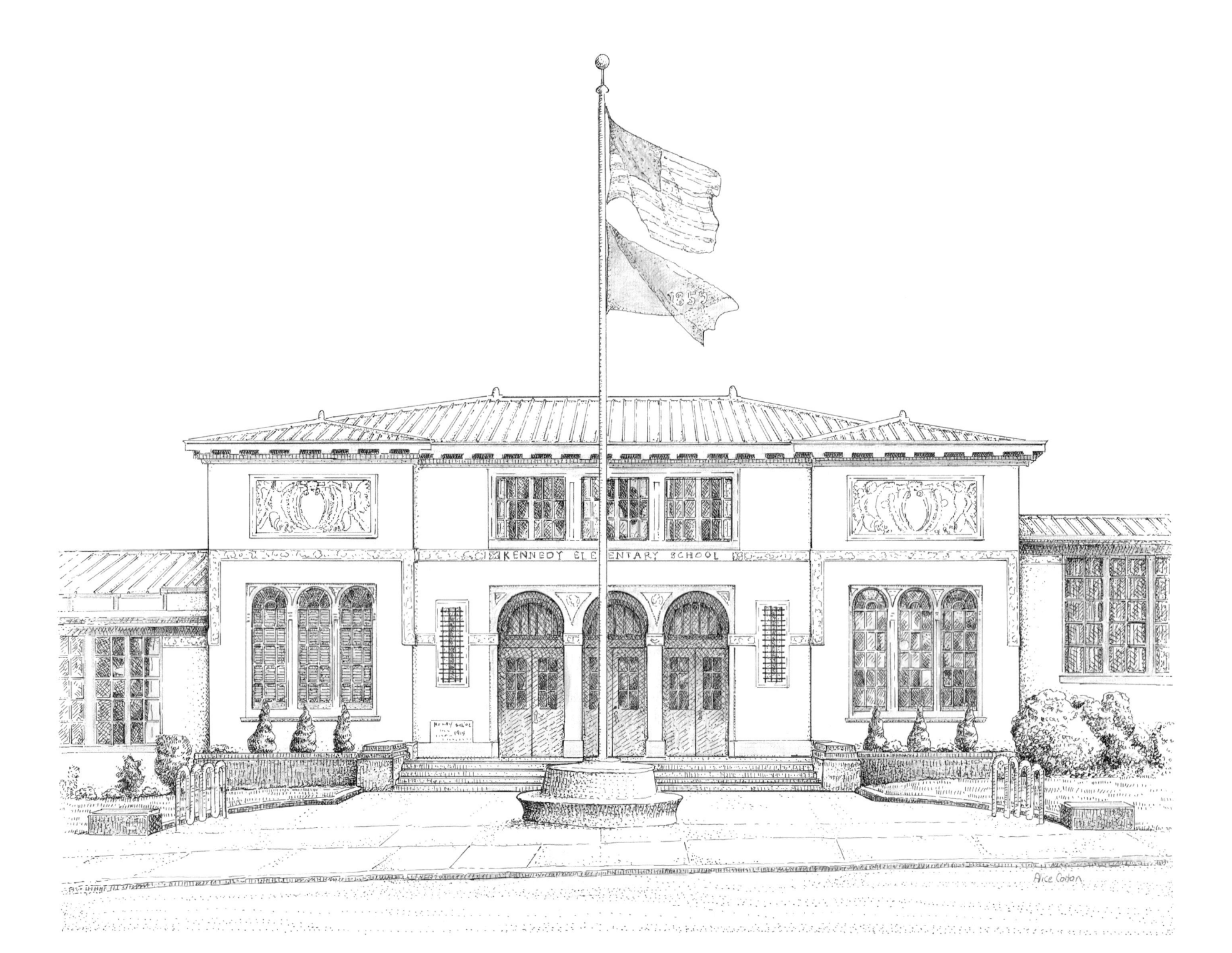

LOCATION: 5736 NE 33rd Avenue, Portland, Oregon

ARCHITECTURAL STYLE: Mediterranean

ARCHITECT: Floyd A. Naramore

DATE BUILT: 1913–15

KENNEDY SCHOOL'S UNIQUE FLOOR PLAN

OWNERS: John Daniel Kennedy was born in Limerick, Ireland. He immigrated to the United States in 1886 and came to Oregon in the mid-1880s where he purchased large parcels of forest and farmland along a county road (present day NE 33rd Avenue). He grew pears and prunes and later became involved in dry goods sales and real estate.

After a devastating economic depression, referred to as the 1893 Panic, most of the city's expansion was halted. John Kennedy helped to revitalize east Portland by donating some of his land for a new Catholic church and selling a four-acre lot to the Portland School District. In order to make room for a new city elementary school, Kennedy was willing to remove his barn, a hen house, and his orchards. Kennedy Elementary School opened in September 1913 and classes were conducted in a portable building until the permanent building was finished. The school was designed to accommodate the growing neighborhood. Classrooms were eventually added until the entire courtyard at the back of the building was completely enclosed. Much later, the school closed due to decreasing enrollment and deterioration, and the building was purchased in 1994 by restaurant owners and entrepreneurs Brian and Mike McMenamin. The McMenamins renovated the school and are currently running it as a bed and breakfast — the complex includes a theater, gymnasium, restaurant, pool, and banquet rooms.

ANECDOTES: Beginning at the turn of the century, there was a tremendous interest in a vast array of revival styles in the United States, including Mediterranean-style architecture. The particular houses that influenced most Mediterranean-style architecture in Portland were those fifteenth- and-seventeenth-century Italian country villas or hill-town dwellings of Tuscany, Venetia, and Lazio (where Rome is located). Mediterranean houses are distinguished by their low-pitched, hipped, terra-cotta tiled roofs, arched entrances, and stuccoed exterior walls. Kennedy School is an example of a symmetrically styled Mediterranean with a recessed entrance and arched openings. Kennedy commissioned the casting of four bas-relief panels, reproductions of fifteenth-century Florentine masterpieces, and several smaller sculpted works. These works were viewed by the public as important contributions of art to Portland's public schools.

The school's single-story plan was an innovation and reflected concerns for school safety and growth. This landmark school design was the creation of Floyd A. Naramore, a Portland School District architect, and was inspired in part by a fatal school fire in Ohio. The design allowed for a much safer evacuation in case of emergency. The school began with twenty-three classrooms, an auditorium, a cafeteria, a gymnasium, two offices, a library, and a boiler room. Classrooms were added as the neighborhood's population grew. These new additions were housed with architectural terra cotta made in strict accordance with detailed drawings that matched the original work. The school featured maple floors, and in each classroom there was a window elevation, a full-width blackboard, four cloak closets, and one bank of bookshelves. The classroom door fronts were covered with black chalkboard.

KENNEDY ELEMENTARY SCHOOL

On NE 33rd Avenue, there is a wonderfully sculpted piece of architecture with rounded arches, a low-sloped roof, decorative relief panels, and a pair of long arms of continuing architecture (not shown here) stretching out from side to side. Within each arm is a hallway that was once lined with children's artwork, state reports, spelling honors, and papier-maché murals. At the end of each arm is a rectangular structure that houses even more classrooms. The sounds of giggling children, crinkling paper, and the ubiquitous scratch of white chalk against the teacher's blackboard echoes ephemeral and ghost-like throughout the school. At the time the school opened, children ate real home-cooked meals, stood in the corner for misbehaving, and posed for pictures for an article in the *Ladies Home Journal* called, "The New One-Story Schoolhouse, Showing the Possibilities of Such Buildings as Developed on the Pacific Coast." Years later, groups of children came each Friday night with their families to see feature films and brought in cans for the "tin can drive" to help support the war effort in 1941. At one time, Martha Rohner, who became a physician, may have come in with her parents to watch them vote; or as a young man, Amo De Bernardis, who became the founding president of Portland Community College, may have volunteered to help the victims of the Vanport flood when the school was set up as a shelter; or perhaps Pete Ward, who became a major league baseball player, had Mrs. Martha Jordan as his music teacher when she became Oregon's first African American teacher at an integrated school. It was an historic school, embraced within nearly a century of memories and shrouded in an exquisitely crafted architecture — a must for this book.

№ 13

42

Hollywood Theatre

LOCATION: 4122 NE Sandy Boulevard, Portland, Oregon

ARCHITECTURAL STYLE: Spanish Baroque with a Byzantine, rococo tower

DATE BUILT: 1923–26

ARCHITECTS: John Virginius Bennes and Herman A. Herzog. John Bennes was trained in Prague, Bohemia, and began his career in Chicago, Illinois. Herman Herzog came from Texas and moved to Portland when he was fifteen years old. Herzog studied architecture at the University of Pennsylvania and worked in Philadelphia and New York before returning to Portland in 1921. He worked as a draftsman in the office of John Bennes and eventually became Bennes's partner. Both architects continued with reputable careers in Portland, even after the dissolution of the Bennes/Herzog partnership.

OWNERS: Claude S. Jensen and John G. von Herberg were prominent theater men on the west coast and were the first to purchase the Hollywood Theatre. They sold the Hollywood Theatre to the North American Theatre Corp. The Hollywood went through several owners until 1975, when the theater was sold to ACT III Theatres. In 1997, the Hollywood Theatre was purchased by the Oregon Film and Video Foundation, which is currently working on a plan to restore the building to its original form. Richard Beer heads the Hollywood Theatre's Restoration Project.

ANECDOTES: The Hollywood was the last theater in Portland built both as a vaudeville and movie house. It opened for business on July 17, 1926, running vaudeville acts, and on Friday nights manager E. E. Marsh allowed audiences an extra bonus—dancing in the balcony to a live orchestra after the show was over. The Hollywood Theatre became so popular that the area around it became known as the Hollywood District.

The Hollywood Theatre was built on a rhomboid-shaped lot that allowed designers to be creative with the building's side elevations (not shown). The ground floor was, and still is, occupied by shops. In keeping with the style of Spanish Baroque, the Hollywood was built with a red-tiled roof and a tinted terra-cotta facade. Above the marquee level, the decorative scheme was elaborately detailed in both eclecticism and terra-cotta styles. The front doors and marquee have been altered over the years.

Around the time the Hollywood Theatre was built, other prominent Portland theaters were being demolished. Theater in Oregon was very popular in the early 1900s and many excellent theater companies thrived in the city of Portland. With the advent of silent movies, however, most theaters were eventually closed down and/or were turned into movie houses, as was the Hollywood. Unfortunately for Portland, the major Portland theater companies of the early 1900s disappeared as career-minded theater people had to go elsewhere to make a living.

The first silent film shown at the Hollywood Theatre was Peter B. Keynes's production of *More Pay-Less Work*. There was an eight-piece orchestra and an organist to accompany the silent films, and a variety of live acts filled out the evening's entertainment. In the 1940s, the theater was the scene of many war bond drives and other civic-oriented causes, as well as many community events. After World War II, there were Saturday morning live radio broadcasts, Halloween spook shows, and many movies. During the 1950s and 60s, the Hollywood, the first cineramic theater in the Pacific Northwest, housed a three-projector-wide screen innovation called "Cinerama." In 1975, the Hollywood Theatre was split into three smaller auditoriums to become a multiplex. The Hollywood slipped into disrepair for a while, operating as a discount ACT III movie house.

This is when the Oregon Film and Video Foundation got involved and purchased the Hollywood Theatre from ACT III Theatres in 1997 for the purpose of preservation and gradual renovation. Volunteers and local businesses helped with the initial clean up of the Hollywood when it was purchased. The Hollywood reopened in November of 1997 and now provides movies, concerts, live performances, and other public and private events under the name of the Hollywood Theatre Project.

The mission of the Film Foundation's Hollywood Theatre Project is to preserve Portland's last grand neighborhood theater and to provide ongoing educational and cultural activities linking Oregon's film, video, and arts communities. The organization is especially interested in premiering films made by Oregonians. The Project is always accepting donations to help with renovation costs. It is a pleasure to visit them at www.hollywoodtheatre.org.

The ornate Hollywood Theatre stands as an appropriately dramatic monument honoring an era when Portland audiences applauded the arrival of live theater and first-run silent movies. It was a time when the Hollywood provided backstage dressing rooms that bustled with actors, comedians, musicians, and dancers. Its hallways were permeated with the smell of nerve-calming liqueurs, flowers, and perfume. You could hear trumpets and violins tuning up for the show and watch with anticipation as the pianist rushed in with a fistful of music while the master of ceremonies announced the silent movie presentation of the evening. The face and detailing of this building fully describe its past life as a vaudeville and movie palace. Its detailing is dramatic and full of surprises. It shows what is possible when one is driven by passion and talent. Its colorful organization and whimsical features beckon us to buy a ticket and go inside. As this theater is one of the last of its kind in Portland, I felt it deserved a place in my book.

Nº 14

44

LOCATION: 2847 SW Westover Road, Portland, Oregon

ARCHITECTURAL STYLE: Georgian Revival

ARCHITECT: Henry C. Dittrich, born in Germany

BUILDERS: Lafayette Pence began and then abandoned the work of the Westover Project, which included the Ashley House. It was completed by a Seattle firm, which worked with John Olmsted, landscape architect, to create Westover Terraces residential neighborhood.

DATE BUILT: 1913

OWNERS: Ladd Estate purchased and may still own the residential area of Westover Terraces where the Ashley House is located, though Mark and Mabel Ashley were the first owners of this particular house. Mark Ashley was the son of English parents who immigrated to New York. Ashley came to Oregon when he was twenty years old, founded a banking house with his brother Rumelin, and did well in the banking business. The Ashley family members remained in this house their entire lives. Thomas J. and Marie Spence owned it when the house was put on the historical register in 1970.

ANECDOTES: Westover Terraces was the vision of Lafayette Pence, who believed using hydraulic power and sluicing methods to terrace Goldsmith Hill would create a special kind of terraced neighborhood where everyone had a beautiful view and a high quality of life. The excess earth and rocks were sent down a flume to the bottom of the hill and filled a lake. Originally the idea was looked upon with skepticism and ridicule. Pence abandoned the project due to financial problems and it was taken over and completed by a Seattle firm (name unknown). John Olmsted developed the idea of serpentine roads weaving up the hill, creating little mini-neighborhoods within the whole, each a little different, which made the area even more special to potential buyers. The homes were large and featured a variety of architectural styles. Ironically, while Pence suffered great humiliation when he first envisioned Westover Terraces and began excavation, when completed Westover Hills was hailed as an engineering marvel and viewed as one of the finest residential areas in the United States.

The Georgian-styled house typically had a rigid rectangular symmetry, geometric proportions, sash windows, two Ionic pilasters, a centered front entrance, and a portico supported by two Ionic columns. The Ashley's widow's walk is balustraded on three sides, and the gable roof features two eyebrow dormers and a hip-roofed dormer. Though unable to tell from the exterior, the house actually has five stories. The clarity of design and harmony of the facade is determined by the classical proportions of the Greek Ionic order.

Three types of columns were developed by the Greeks: Doric, Ionic, and Corinthian. They each signified specific mathematical proportions and ornamentation called an "order." The ancient Romans further developed this mode of construction

THE MARK ASHLEY HOUSE

The Ashley House takes the idea of classical order and symmetry and projects it boldly with its huge Ionian columns and pilasters, which are sharply contrasted by the deeply recessed portico. The dauntless facade of the Ashley House is greatly softened by the two sleepy eyes of its eyebrow dormers. Most interestingly, this lovely creation is part of a much larger picture — an innovative neighborhood presiding in the Westover Hills section of the city of Portland. I had to drive up a series of winding roads to find the Ashley House where it stands overlooking the city. There were several large trees directly in front of the building that I "moved" to the sides so my readers could see the entire building. I expanded the view of the Willamette River valley to include an older version of Portland behind the house so as to demonstrate the original, intended effect more succinctly. The Ashley's Georgian Revival design is a sister architecture to the other revived classical styles constructed in the early 1900s.

№ 15

in their religious, military, civil, and engineering structures, adding two further types of columns: the Tuscan and the Composite. The Romans also enriched the repertoire of architectural form by creating the arch, the dome, and the vault.

Georgian Revival became popular in England during the time of the four King Georges. They were built in large numbers in America in the 1700s and 1800s.

46

LOCATION: 841 South Promenade, Seaside, Oregon

ARCHITECTURAL STYLE: Bungalow

DATE BUILT: 1925

OWNERS: This vacation house was built for Harry Haller, executive of the Kelley Clarke Lumber Company in Portland, Oregon. In 1933, Haller turned over the title of this house to Marie Sealy and Helen Black. Sealy relinquished her part of the property to Helen and Harvey Black, who resided in Portland and used this house as their vacation retreat.

ANECDOTES: The Haller-Black House is a prime example of an early vacation home along the Oregon coast at Seaside. Seaside was, and still is, one of Oregon's most popular coastal resorts. Seaside's name came from a famous hotel resort, the Seaside House, which was located at the designated end of the Lewis and Clark Trail. Seaside's development was sporadic until the Columbia River Railroad established itself. This brought a great surge of tourism and a boom in the construction of recreational housing. The promenade was constructed along the beachfront, replacing a wooden boardwalk. The "Prom" provides scenic views of the coast, and it links the dwellings along the eastern side. Most of these buildings were constructed before 1935.

The original concept for the bungalow came from India and referred to one-story houses with steep, long, overhanging rooflines that were built to protect British colonists from the heat and harsh sun. England borrowed the style, and it became the symbol of an unpretentious lifestyle. In America, small one-story Queen-Anne-styled cottages grew in popularity in California in the 1880s and 1890s. Later, as the Queen Anne influences were abandoned, a less ornate style of bungalow began to appear. At first, the bungalow was viewed as strictly a vacation home — a summer residence that harmonized with its natural surroundings and that was set up for rustic living. Later, as bungalows began to become more popular in the United States, they were transformed into permanent housing in urban development areas. The very popular "love of cottage" sentiment of the early 1900s brought about a burgeoning of bungalow development throughout the United States. It was the bungalow form of practical, mass-produced homes that launched the American suburb, reaching its peak in the 1920s. The bungalow symbolized a protest to the rapid pace and technological predominance of modern life.

The Haller-Black House features the Bungalow style, with its steeply pitched roof with deep eaves and exposed rafters. The wood shingles that layer the roof and siding are a particularly striking feature found in many Bungalow-styled buildings. The *Craftsman Magazine* and other builders' journals in the early 1900s influenced the building of a great many Bungalow-styled homes in the United States. Bungalow architecture represented an American movement towards providing distinctive quality housing for anyone with the desire to build a home.

THE HALLER-BLACK HOUSE

White sand and the salty smell of ocean greeted my sister and I as we stepped onto the stony walkway of the Seaside Promenade. The soothing roar of the Pacific Ocean slowed us down long enough to take notice of a long, steeply pitched roof of a Seaside bungalow. The roof covered every floor in such a way that you could imagine feeling cozy and hidden within it. Of course it might have been the fact that the Haller-Black House was surounded by the natural hues and textures of aging wood and brick that caught our attention. But, upon reflection, I believe this veteran of raging winds and coastal thunderstorms beckoned us because it needed an audience; for painted on its vast array of wooden shingles was a deeply passionate work revealing an art well-disciplined in the ancient science of natural weathering. As my sister left to take a closer look at the ocean, I photographed the Haller-Black bungalow and promised it a place in my book.

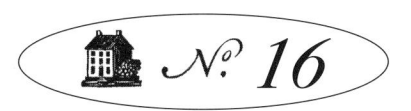

N° 16

Bungalows were influenced by a wide variety of architectural styles, including Swiss Chalet, English Cottage, Colonial, Spanish, and Japanese. Most bungalows had widely extended eaves, one or one-and-a-half stories, wood shingles, stone or brick foundations, banks of casement windows, and a predominant porch, often across the entire front of the house. They embraced an "open planning" philosophy, using natural materials and simplicity of detail. Gustav Stickley, the man whose energy fueled the *Craftsman Magazine*, promoted these styles by including plans, drawings, and instructions. Stickley also made furniture, which was shown in the magazine as well. The *Craftsman Magazine* gave step-saving advice, space-saving tips, and outlined low-cost features.

48

LOCATION: Highway 101, Garibaldi, Oregon

ARCHITECTURAL STYLE: Maritime Colonial Revival

DESIGNERS: The Coast Guard's Chief Civil Engineer's Office in Washington D. C.

DATE BUILT: 1942

OWNERS: The United States Coast Guard. This particular building is the home of the executive petty officer, Chief Jon Gagnon, and his family, as well as the operations officer, Petty Officer Speer. Officer-in-charge, Master Chief Kent, lives in a house on the grounds, and there is a barracks in the back that houses many of the other officers who serve at the Tillamook Bay Station.

ANECDOTES: Typical of Colonial Revival buildings, this one has a symmetrical composition, a central hall plan, gable roofs with molded cornices, dark painted wood shutters, a porch with Tuscan columns, and a balustrade with short columns that match those of the porch below. The Colonial style was popular during the 1930s throughout the United States and was often favored for the design of government buildings.

The Roman republican architect and engineer, Vitruvius, wrote that there were three principles to the art of architecture: the building's function (*utilitas*), its structure (*firmitas*), and its design (*venustas*). The Tillamook Bay Coast Guard Station demonstrates how these three elements work together when the building's designers integrated the idea of a functional semi-military government guardhouse at a coastal location with the formal structure and aesthetic of Colonial Revival architecture. This created a unique Colonial Revival style appropriately coined "Maritime Colonial Revival."

This Coast Guard station began its service in 1907, when the Coast Guard was called the "Life-Saving Service." In 1915, the "Coast Guard" became the name of the federal service whose primary mission was to save lives at sea. It is interesting to note that during World War II, the Tillamook Bay Coast Guard Station was part of a national mobilization effort for the defense of the Pacific coast during World War I when it grew to over 240,000 personnel and fought in all areas of the war. The Coast Guard responded to the national state of emergency that went into effect following Roosevelt's declaration of war in 1939 until the surrender of the Japanese in the Pacific in 1945.

With the threat of attack during World War II, the personnel of the Tillamook station were asked to expand their duties to include the operation of wartime beach patrols. All coastal areas of the United States were organized into defense divisions known as Naval Coastal Frontiers armed with army and navy personnel committed to guarding the coast against invasion. The wartime beach patrols had three basic functions: to detect and observe enemy vessels and transmit information to the appropriate navy and army commands, to report attempted enemy landings, and to prevent communication between persons on shore and the enemy at sea. The patrol also functioned as a rescue agency and policed restricted areas of the coast. The crew at the Tillamook Bay Station, which overlooks Tillamook Bay, was

TILLAMOOK BAY COAST GUARD STATION

I had seen a picture of this beautiful Colonial Revival in one of my research books, and I was sure I wanted to see it. When I did, it was sitting peacefully along the coastal waters of Tillamook Bay. The three alert, watchful eyes of its roof dormers peered through the coastal fog to watch over the bay, much as its beach patrol officers did many years ago. I was gratified to see the station's watchtower cupola keeping constant surveillance over our coastal waters. The building's brick foundation and the extended wings on either side gave it a look of stability that I found comforting. The station appeared to be an ethical, predictable architecture built to function, like its human counterparts, as a trusted guardian of our well-being and way of life.

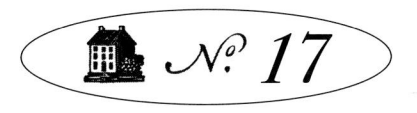

N° 17

responsible for checking each entering or departing vessel. All bays and harbors were considered important to the coastal defense effort. The beach patrols along the Pacific Northwest coastline were facilitated by the existence of a system of coastal lookouts, established in 1941, along the Oregon and Washington coasts. In 1942, the Oregon/Washington coast had thirteen lifeboat stations with continuous lookouts at harbor entrances and twenty-six coastal lookout stations strategically located to cover areas where enemy forces could most easily infiltrate. Each station had a twenty-four hour watch. When the war was over, these beach patrols were discontinued.

Since World War II, the Coast Guard returned to its original mission as a search-and-rescue operation in the service of saving lives at sea, law enforcement, and maritime environmental pollution response. The Coast Guard is involved in training its officers for medical emergencies and rescue operations at sea. Over its many years of service, the United States Coast Guard emphasizes beach safety and is on call for such things as capsized boats, swimmers and boatsman who are lost or in trouble, freak wave disasters, water sports accidents, and flood-stranded people.

50

LOCATION: 533 Lincoln Street South (the corner of Lincoln and John Streets), Salem, Oregon

ARCHITECTURAL STYLE: Twentieth-Century English Tudor Revival

DESIGNER: Ellis Lawrence

DATE BUILT: 1923–24

ARCHITECTS: The Ellis F. Lawrence and William G. Holford architectural firm. Ellis Lawrence was the principal designer and is thought to have been responsible for nearly all the firm's designs. William Holford's role was design development, and it is thought that he was responsible for much of the landscaping for the firm's projects. Within the firm's body of work, 199 residences have been identified. Nine of these have been classified as Tudor.

OWNERS: Thomas Albert Livesley and family were the first owners of this mansion. Thomas Livesley was a progressive mayor of Salem from 1927 until 1931 and a state legislator from 1937 through 1939. His primary emphasis as mayor was on the construction of permanent concrete bridges and the paving of streets, alleys, and sidewalks "in the interest of economy and civic beauty." Livesley's tenure also included the building of two new fire stations, the Salem airport, a refuse incinerator plant, the installation of street lights, three new playgrounds, a traffic signal system, a building inspection department, and the adoption of uniform building, electric, and plumbing codes. Livesley made improvements in running the city government and gave the city a more businesslike administration.

Livesley was a noted philanthropist and civic leader. Livesley and his wife, Edna, played a prominent social role in their community. They included the designation of a formal "Reception Room" in the architectural plan of the house. This was considered unusual for the particular plans they used. The Livesley House was the site of many charity teas for such organizations as the hospital, symphony, various children's causes and so on. Edna Livesley oversaw these fundraising events.

Before Livesley became a politician, he was a very successful, world-renowned hops grower and broker. Livesley played an important role in the promotion and development of the Oregon hop industry. He was a leader at the forefront of social reform for the welfare of workers in the hops fields and an innovator in the practice of the latest scientific and technical advances in hop agriculture in the state.

In 1988, the state of Oregon purchased the Livesley mansion and made it the Governor's mansion. In 1989, the house was designated a local historic landmark, and in 1990, the Livesley House was placed on the *National Register of Properties*. The first governor to reside in the Livesley House was Governor Neil Goldschmidt and his family.

ANECDOTES: Tudor-styled houses are typically asymmetrical with an entrance hall and an entrance portico that are centrally located and prominently featured. Tudor roofs are steeply pitched and the siding features the use of half-timbering with brick, stone, stucco, and beveled shiplap siding. Tudors used an abundance of windows

THE LIVESLEY HOUSE
GOVERNOR'S RESIDENCE

Neatly tucked away behind a secured iron gate and a perimeter of shrubs, bushes, and iron fencing, I found this magnificent English Tudor mansion. I couldn't get into the yard to take my photos, so I crawled into the bushes and photographed the house through a gap in the fence. This seemed a good idea until I realized that this was, after all, the governor's home, and my sneaking around the property could get me arrested. But, I could not leave. My passion to include this house in my book overcame me, or perhaps it was the pleasant smell of the surrounding foliage that kept me from moving. So I stayed put until I noticed a security guard walking across the gardens. I quickly got up to meet him at the front gate. I proceeded to explain myself and to demonstrate how incredibly harmless I was, when he kindly interrupted my effusing and said that I could finish my photo session. He suggested that I do it quickly, though, for I was apparently making "everyone nervous inside" as a number of alarms had been set off. "Please tell them I'm just an artist who loves their house! And that I'm not a threatening person and I'm writing a book and . . . ," I called pathetically after him as he made his way back towards the mansion. He smiled and waved. Silly me.

№ 18

with multipaned casements and wide polygonal bays. A feature called the Tudor arch is also a distinctive Tudor attribute and is usually found in and around the doorways. The Tudor style originated in England where the streets were narrow. Because of the prominent use of cantilevered second floors for additional floor space, whole towns were designed in the Tudor style.

52

LOCATION: 1728 SW Prospect Drive, Portland, Oregon

ARCHITECTURAL STYLE: Colonial Revival

ARCHITECT: David C. Lewis, David Honeyman's brother-in-law, was a celebrated, native-born architect who trained at Columbia University. He also attended Princeton University and designed a number of noteworthy buildings in Portland.

DATE BUILT: 1907–8

OWNERS: The house was built for David Honeyman and his wife, known as Nan Wood. Nan Wood was noted as a progressive leader and reformer in the political arena during the 1920s. She served as president of the League of Women Voters and as the state and national committee woman for the Democratic party. She was elected president of the Oregon division of the Woman's National Organization for Prohibition Reform, a group which sought an end to prohibition. The organization ran head-to-head with its powerful rival, the Woman's Christian Temperance Union. However, the support to end prohibition proved strong and, in 1933, Wood was elected president of the Constitutional Convention, which ratified the Twenty-First Amendment, repealing prohibition.

Nan Wood was also elected to the Oregon legislature and was the first woman to be elected to the U.S. Congress as a representative from Oregon's third district. She campaigned for a seat in the U.S. House of Representatives by running on the New Deal platform. Wood won the election and went to Washington with her daughter, Judith. Her husband, David Honeyman, stayed home to take care of the family business.

Nan Wood was a strong supporter of the New Deal and a personal friend to President and Eleanor Roosevelt. Wood met Eleanor Roosevelt at Finche School in New York, where Wood studied music. The two became good friends, and Eleanor Roosevelt was often Nan's guest.

Nan Wood was a proactive leader and served on the Rivers and Harbors Committee, the Irrigation and Reclamation Committee, and the Committee on Indian Affairs. She worked to control the pollution of the Columbia River and to protect the salmon fishing industry. She was interested in the development of the Columbia River as a major waterway and was an outspoken advocate for the construction of transmission lines to carry power throughout the Pacific Northwest. Wood was also interested in the enactment of the Federal Old Age Pension Plan and in veteran's legislation.

David Honeyman's family owned the largest hardware store in Portland, where David was vice president and treasurer. He was also director of the Portland Gas and Coal Company and an officer of the Electric Products Corporation.

In the early 60s, the Honeymans sold their house to James Gilbert Robbins Jr. and his wife, Helen Wall Robbins. In 1989, John Watson and Patricia Palmer bought the house from the Robbins.

ANECDOTES: The classical elements of the Honeyman-Wood House design are finely detailed, particularly the six colossal, fluted Corinthian columns. The entablature includes architrave, frieze, and an end cornice and is crowned with an attic balustrade over the portico. It is rectangular in mass with a low-pitched, truncated hip roof. It is made of wood construction. The Colonial Revival, which embraced the traditions of classical architecture, symbolized restraint, order, and elegance. The architectural forms came from classic Greek, Roman, and Renaissance traditions.

In the southeast corner of the property is a giant sequoia tree. It has been said that Colonel L. L. Hawkins, founding member of the Mazamas and influential outdoorsman, had given the sequoia to the Honeymans. Upon his death, the Honeyman-Woods considered the sequoia to be a living memorial to their neighbor and friend.

The grounds also contain many ornamental plants common to the urban landscape of the Pacific Northwest. For example, there is a Kwanzan flowering cherry, a large English holly tree, azaleas, rhododendrons, hydrangeas, dogwoods, boxwoods, skimmias, and camellias.

THE DAVID T. HONEYMAN AND NAN WOOD HOUSE

Strikingly beautiful and ultimately classic in design, this Colonial Revival left me awestruck. I found myself as overwhelmed by the grandeur of its Corinthian columns as I was by the woman who once lived within it, Nan Wood. The early Greeks sought to establish a purity of form and an adherence to a natural order by articulating the kind of architecture that is portrayed in the Honeyman-Wood House. Nan Wood sought to make a positive difference in the world by creating a political career based on a platform of equality for all people and environmental awareness—an unusual role for women in the early 1900s. Together, both the woman and the house made a powerful package: breathtaking and noble. I had to photograph the house several times to find an angle that would offer the most dramatic view of this building's size and aura. I also wanted to include some of the many wonderful trees that have grown on the property since the house was first built. For example, there is a very large sequoia tree in the front that you can see on the left side of the picture and again towering overhead at the top.

N.º 19

54

LOCATION: 2526 St. Helen's Court, Portland, Oregon

ARCHITECTURAL STYLE: English Cottage in the style of the Arts and Crafts tradition

CONTRACTOR: N. J. Nelson

DATE BUILT: 1923

ARCHITECT: Wade Pipes, brother of George Pipes who owned the house, was born in Independence, Oregon, and became a prominent Portland architect. He was Oregon's leading exponent of the English Arts and Crafts movement. Wade studied in England and absorbed the works of the leading architects in the Arts and Crafts movement in London.

Wade Pipes loved to draw and kept a sketch book at his side at all times. He was an avid gardener and often designed gardens for his clients as an integral part of the house design. "Wade Pipes was a man out of his time; a free spirit living in an uneasy truce with a technologically obsessed society. He began as a skillful craftsman and became an inspired designer with a flair for good composition and fine detailing, uncompromising in his principles and adamant in what he thought to be appropriate and beautiful" (Belluschi ix). Pipes displays his sensitivity to the landscape and surrounding environment by the incorporation of a transitional rear porch and patio that opens to a terraced backyard (not shown), reminiscent of an English garden design. Wade also designed natural linen curtains for the Pipes home. These were hand embroidered by his wife, Genevieve, and her sister, Dorothy.

Wade and Genevieve both loved the arts, which were an integral part of their lives. Genevieve Frazer Pipes came from a musically gifted family. She studied piano in Vienna and taught private piano lessons for many years. Her sister, Dorothy, married George Pipes, the owner of this house.

OWNERS: George Pipes, brother to Wade Pipes, was a prominent Portland attorney. He served as chief civil deputy district attorney for Multnomah County and as a government attorney for the Bonneville Dam Administration and the United States Engineers. George Pipes also served as bar examiner under appointment by the Oregon Supreme Court. Pipes was known for collecting rare books and became an authority on ancient Greek and Roman coins. He, like his brother Wade, loved gardens and gardening. George married Dorothy Frazer, who remained very close to her sister, Genevieve, and the two couples spent much time together sharing conversation, meals, and listening to music. George and Dorothy had two children, Mary and John.

ANECDOTES: The Pipes House is symmetrical in plan and has one dramatic sweeping gable roof. The single gable is unlike Wade Pipes's characteristic roof line, which often had many gables. The roof forms a beautiful semicircular figure on the front and rear elevations and is a dominant feature in the design.

Arts-and-Crafts-styled houses usually featured multiple steeply pitched

THE GEORGE PIPES HOUSE

The Pipes House opened its sleepy eyea when it saw me standing before it. It awoke from its late afternoon snooze and winked at me through the many reflections and shadowy shapes the sun was making as it streamed through the trees above. Leaves and tree branches, both living and shadowed, were spread across the house's roof, the sidewalks, and the paved street. From within its caringly landscaped hillside, the Pipes House seemed to hug me with its circular swayed roof. It looked intimately cozy and snug within the natural world that embraced it. The Pipes House, to me, represents a real Arts and Crafts success story, where house and nature have been blended together by a skillful and sensitive architectural artist.

№ 20

gables, elongated eaves with upper roofs often extended to cover first floor open porches, and stucco or brick siding often combined with wood siding or board and battens. The windows were generally small-scale casements with little or no trim.

In the early 1900s, an Arts and Crafts movement was embraced and was represented by a revitalization of traditional crafts as well as by a proliferation of vernacular architecture that invited one to live closer to one's natural surroundings. The spirit of high quality craftsmanship was encouraged in the face of a technological paradigm that seemed to ostracize the arts in favor of rational science. Individuals and organizations were fighting to keep the equally important creative aspect of being human alive as society continued to trek through its technological era. They warned that losing sight of who we are as creative beings could be our undoing.

Closing

"Architecture is a thing of art, a phenomenon of the emotions. . . .
The purpose of . . . architecture [is] to move us."

Le Corbusier, *Vers une Architecture*

    What better building to end with than a lovely little English Cottage resting on a high slope within a circle of flowers and trees. It is a unique place, where architect, architecture, garden, and homeowner were once unified in creating a beautiful, harmonious environment in which to live. The buildings in this book, and other historical buildings similar to these, represent the quintessential blending of the arts and sciences; they provide an invaluable link between ancient and modern humans; and they exemplify what it is to live in a society that views both its art and its technology as inseparable, as equal partners in the founding of a sanctuary we call home.

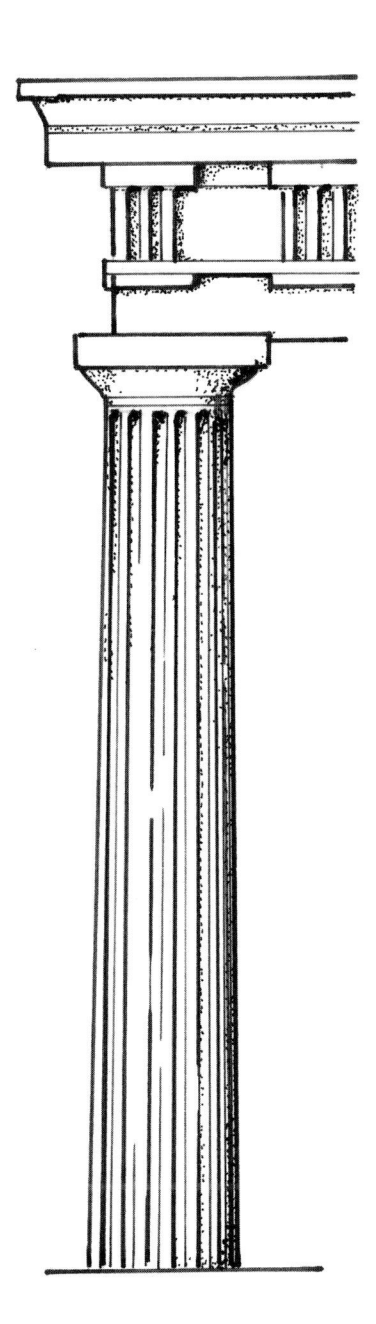

APPENDIX

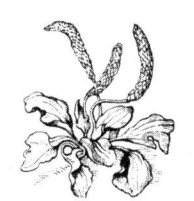

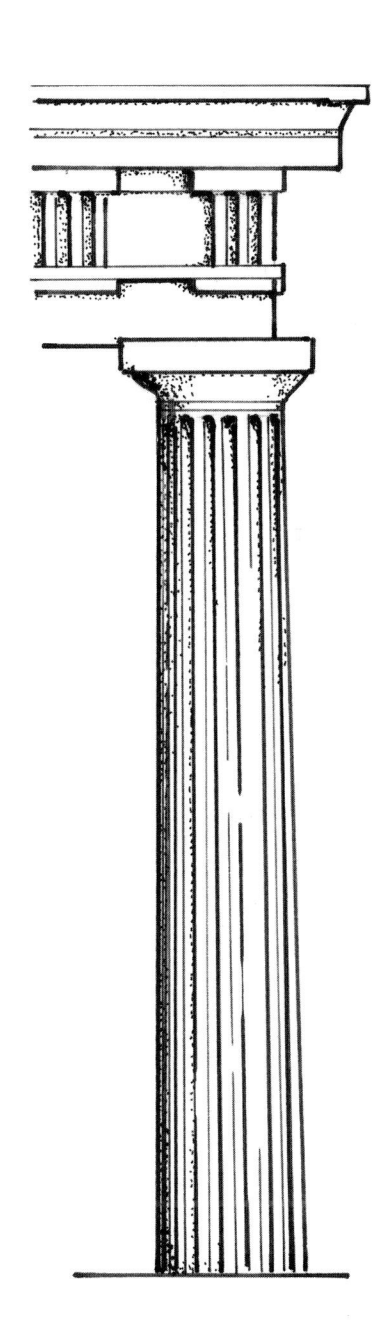

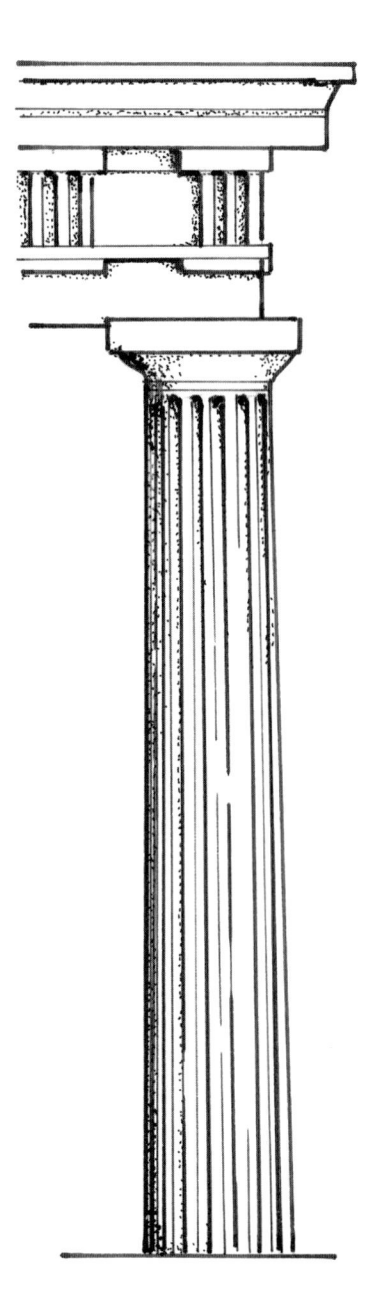

AN EXAMPLE OF A DORIC COLUMN

The Doric Order of Greek Architecture

Vitruvius, a Roman architect, was the first person to publish a book on architecture. His *Ten Books on Architecture* was written during the time of Augustus (27 B.C.–A.D. 14). In his book, Vitruvius made a study of Greek architecture, where he outlined the principles and proportions of Greek temple construction, including the Doric, Ionic, and Corinthian orders. Many Colonial Revival and Greek Revival architectural styles outlined in this book used columns and entablatures based upon ancient Greek and Roman architecture.

The Greeks believed that proportion was as essential in providing beauty and harmony between the parts of a building as it was in providing beauty and harmony in the human figure. The first and oldest of the three Greek orders, the Doric order, was built according to proportions based on the male human figure. Like the average male figure, the width of the column (a man's foot length) was considered one-sixth and then later one-seventh of the column's (man's) height. Doric columns were sturdy and basic in construction, they did not have a base, and their capitals were rectangular and unadorned. The earliest Doric temples were made of wood, and it is believed by some sources that the wooden entablatures and the columns that supported them were eventually replaced with stone as the wood decayed. Whether used as a replacement material or whether first used as materials in their own right, stone and marble buildings were constructed in the form of the early post-and-lintel timber buildings.

The word "Doric" is derived from the name of a king, Dorus, who, according to Greek legend, was the son of Hellen and the nymph Phthia. It was believed that Dorus built the first Doric temple.

The Ionic Order of Greek Architecture

The Ionic order was a variant of the Doric order and used the female human figure as the standard: the foot of a woman, or width of the column, was considered one-eighth — later one-ninth — the vertical length of the column or female figure. Ionic columns were slender and graceful with dentils decorating their cornices. Ionian columns had pedestals, and volutes were added to the Ionian capital, giving it the look of graceful curling hair. Ionic column shafts were fluted, mimicking the folds on a woman's garment.

The word "Ionic" comes from a part of the world originally composed of thirteen pre-Greek colonies in Asia Minor that united under the name of their leader, Ion. They originally built temples in the Doric order and later developed the Ionic order.

One of the most celebrated Ionic temples during Greek times was the one dedicated to the goddess Artemis (Diana in Roman mythology).

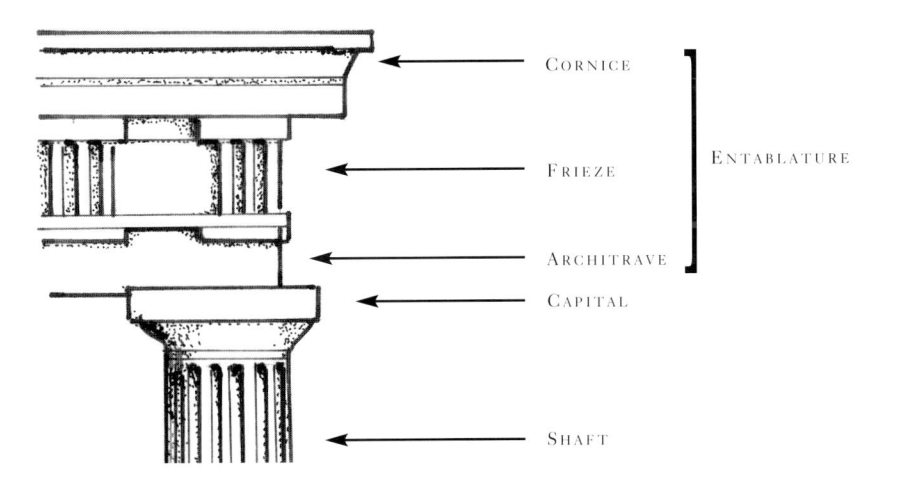

An example of an Ionian column

The Golden Rectangle

The golden rectangle, the golden mean, the golden section, the divine proportion, and the golden ratio are all name variants of a common set of proportions that mysteriously unite mathematics with the occurrence of certain natural phenomenon. The Greeks considered these golden proportions to be both perfect and mystical and used them to design their most sacred architectural and sculptural works. These divine proportions were discovered to be predictable patterns in nature, as witnessed in the spirals of the nautilus shell, starfish, sand dollars, seed head arrangements, pine cones, and pineapples. As you can see below, the golden rectangle can be divided within itself using the golden mean or ratio in such a way as to create a dynamic spiraling effect.

It is interesting to note that the Greeks held that mathematics fell into two categories: (1) utilitarian mathematics, considered a lower form of mathematics, and (2) the number systems of harmony and the patterns of geometry and music, considered the higher branch of mathematics. Harmonious proportions were such an essential component of Greek culture that architects were encouraged to study music to help them create harmonious and beautiful architectural works.

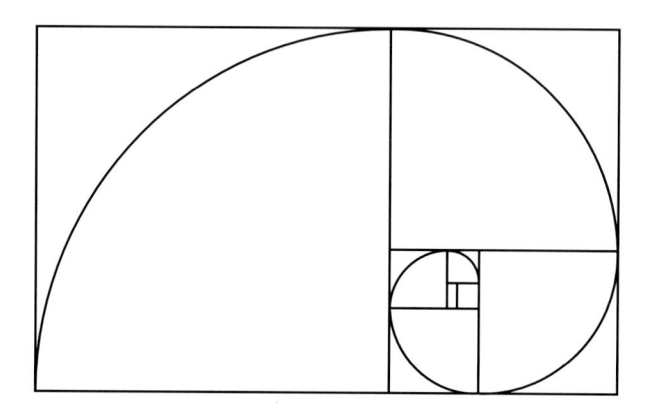

For over 2000 years, architects and artists have been fond of the GOLDEN RECTANGLE, where the length is divided by the width equalling approximately 1.618, a number called the GOLDEN RATIO.

The Greek letter phi ϕ is the symbol for the GOLDEN MEAN (see bottom right).

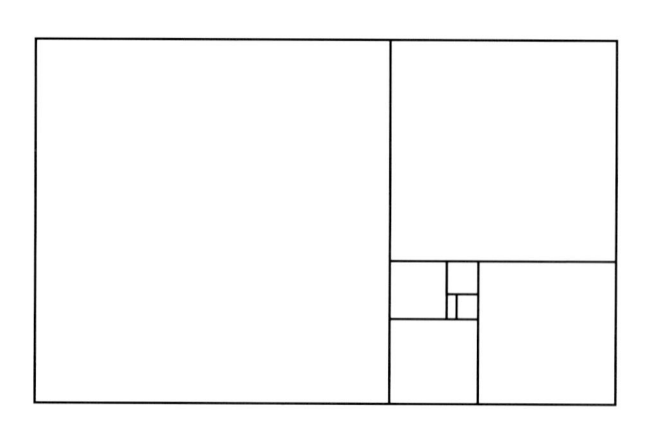

The GOLDEN SECTION — each dimension is 1.618 times the next smaller dimension.

This dynamic spiraling effect found in nature demonstrates the power and beauty of the GOLDEN MEAN.

The GOLDEN MEAN is a proportion that refers to a segment:

A   B   C

such that $\dfrac{|AC|}{|AB|} = \dfrac{|AB|}{|BC|}$

equalling $(1+\sqrt{5})/2 = 1.618$

Special Quotes

"You want to be connected . . . that's the center of the whole thing. When you can start with the history, especially with a school where you have a lot of good vibes coming out of it already, and if you are able to figure out a re-use for it, what you get is the best of all worlds—the past meeting the future. You are continuing in this historical parade. It's a great thing."

Mike McMenamin talking about the McMenamin's historical renovation projects, including Kennedy Elementary School

---

"I've been a part of the Hollywood Theatre Project since our foundation took over operations in August of 1997. A building like this gets in your blood and consumes your life. But each time I see the theater's terra-cotta tower, I know that all the work is worth it—that I'm helping to preserve a very important part of Portland's history."

Richard Beer, director of programming & operations, Hollywood Theatre Project

---

"Oh my God, I grew up in that house! My room was right there where Eleanore Roosevelt used to stay when she visited the Honeymans."

Liz Robbins, general manager of Kennedy School, looking at the Honeyman-Wood House

---

"I have a great uncle who was a neighbor and friend of the Honeymans. He was an influential man, a naturalist, and very good friends with naturalist John Muir and the planners of several Portland improvement projects, the Olmstead Brothers. It is a little-known fact that my uncle is the person who was responsible for bringing the great sequoia trees to Portland."

William Hawkins III, architect, owner of the Kamm House

"I'll never forget the first time I saw the inside of the Barlow House. I had knocked on the door, and the owner, a little lady named Mrs. Page, invited me in. When I stepped inside the entryhall, I had a very strange feeling which made me lean back against the front door. Was it simply amazement at the elegance of the open stairway or was it just that I felt I had lived here before?"

Virginia Miller, owner of the Barlow House

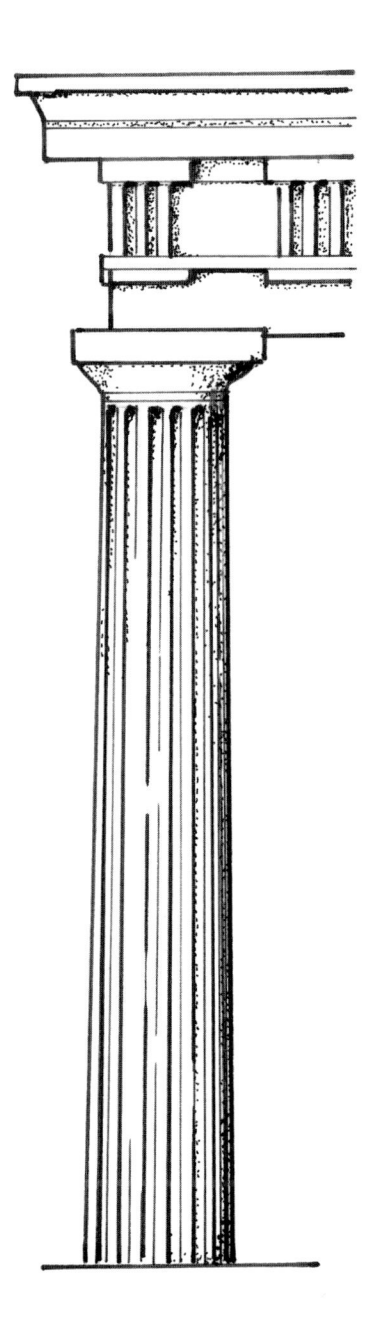

GLOSSARY

BIBLIOGRAPHY

INDEX

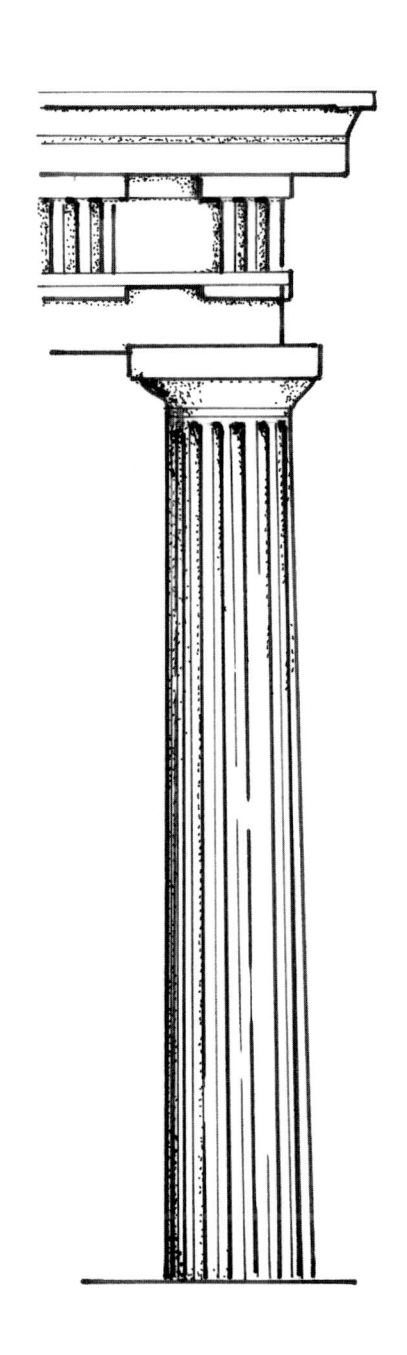

Glossary

Acanthus leaves: A plant found in the Mediterranean. Its leaves have many narrow, pointed lobes and are sometimes spiny. Ancient Greeks and Romans formalized its leaf patterns and used them for decorative purposes.

Acroterion: An ornament that crowns a pediment.

Alberti, Leone Battista (1404–72): The influential Italian architect and theorist who produced the first architectural treatise of the Renaissance. He focused on proportion, the orders, and town planning.

Anthemion: A Greek ornament based on honeysuckle or palmetto motifs.

Arch: A curved, flat, or pointed structure used to span an opening.

Architrave: The lowest part of an entablature; the main beam resting on the top of a column.

Arts and Crafts movement (1895–1988): A revival of traditional crafts and vernacular architecture in the second half of the nineteenth century in Europe and the United States. It was inspired by the ideas of John Ruskin, William A. Morris, and other architects and designers who sought creativity and originality through a return to traditional materials and techniques, honesty in design, and joy in high standards of craft work.

Ashlar masonry: Masonry formed of square or rectangular stones.

~

Balloon frame construction: A building construction method that has vertical wall members that extend uninterrupted from the foundation to the roof.

Baluster: Any of the small posts that support the upper rail of a railing, as in a staircase.

Balustrade: A series of balusters connected by a top rail or hand rail, as on staircases, balconies, or porches; also, the railing connecting the balusters.

Bargeboard: An ornamental board placed on the incline of a gable to conceal rafter ends.

Baroque: The style of art and architecture that emerged in Italy and later spread throughout Europe during the seventeenth century. It was characterized by dynamic lines and masses. It used classical detailing freely.

Battlement: A low wall originally built for defense at the top of a tower or indented parapet used for ornament.

Bay window: A windowed alcove with perpendicular or angled sides that extends out from the exterior wall of a room and is supported by a foundation attached to the house.

Belt cornice: The exterior trim located between floors, similar to a roof cornice but smaller.

Board and batten: Vertical wood siding with thin strips (battens) that extend over adjacent boards or joints.

Bracket: A projecting support that is plain or decorative.

Buttress: A support built against a wall or building to support it.

~

Cantilever: A beam or other projecting structure from a wall and supported at only one end. It serves as an extension to a building.

Capital: The upper portion of a column on which lies the entablature.

Casement: A window frame that opens on vertical hinges containing two vertically hung windows separated by a mullion.

Casing: The visible molding or framework around an opening, such as a door or window.

Clapboard: A long, narrow board having one edge thicker than the other, covering the outer walls of frame structures; also called weatherboard.

Classical: An architectural style or artifact that pertains to the architecture of ancient Greece and Rome.

Colossal order: Columns of any order that are more than one story in height.

Columns: A vertical, usually circular pillar. Columns are used structurally to support a lintel or beam and are associated with a superstructure or the entablature of a particular design. This together with the column is called an order. Each order (see Orders) is also associated with an identifiable standard treatment of the windows, doors, opening, moldings, and ornament of the building in which they are are used. The Classical style is also associated with symmetry, proportion, and a harmonious relationship between the elements that comprise the building. Some classical buildings employ one order, others may employ several orders.

Composite order: A Roman addition to the Greek orders, where the capital combines Ionic volutes with the Corinthian acanthus.

Corbel: A bracket of stone, wood, or other material, on the side of a wall. It helps to support a projecting ledge.

Corinthian order: The most ornate and slender order with two rows of acanthus leaves in a bell-shaped capital.

Corner board: A narrow vertical board at the corner of a traditional wood frame building into which the clapboards butt.

Cornice: The upper projection of a classical entablature; an ornamental molding that projects along the top of a wall, pillar, or side of a building.

Cresting/ridge roll: A decorative ridge at the top of a roof.

Cross gable: A gable that is perpendicular to the main gable or ridge of a roof.

Cupola: A small domelike structure on top of a roof or tower.

~

Dentils: The square blocks under cornices and moldings.

Donation Land Claim Act of 1850: This law gave each white male citizen over the age of eighteen who settled in Oregon before December 1, 1851, 320 acres of land if he was single and 640 acres if he was married.

Doric order: A classical order characterized by a heavily fluted column, a plain capital, and no pedestal. It is the simplest of Greek orders.

Dormer: A window projecting from the slope of a roof with slopes of its own.

~

Eaves: These are the lowest overhanging underparts of a sloping roof.

Entablature: In classical architecture, this is the part of a building supported by the columns and composed of the cornice, frieze, and architrave.

Eyebrow dormer: A dormer that has a rounded roof, resembling an eyelid in appearance.

~

Facade: A principal face or elevation of a building, usually the front.

Facade dormer: A dormer whose front face is an extension of a facade wall.

Fanlight: A window, often semicircular, over a door with radiating muntins suggesting a fan.

Fluting: Vertical grooves or concave channels, as on fluted columns or pilasters.

Formal architecture: This style exhibits a form that is balanced, symmetrical, and regular.

Frame structure: Any building carried on a frame as distinct from load bearing walls.

French doors: Two light doors, composed of small panes of glass, set within rectangular muntins, mounted within one frame and hinged. Usually they open to an outside terrace or porch.

Frieze: The middle section of a classical entablature; also, a decorative horizontal band along the wall or a room.

Gable: The portion above the eaves' level of an end wall of a building with a pitched roof. In the case of a pitched roof, the gable is triangular in form. The term sometimes refers to the entire end wall.

Gable roof: An inverted "V" shaped roof of varying pitches.

Gambrel roof: A roof with a double slope on each of its two sides; typical of Dutch Colonial architecture.

Gingerbread: A pierced, curvilinear ornament made with a jigsaw or scroll saw, predominant in Gothic Revival.

Golden ratio/golden mean/golden rectangle/golden section: The geometric proportion that results when a straight line is divided in such a way that the shorter part is to the longer part as the longer part is to the whole. The golden section was first formulated by Euclid and as been used widely in art and architecture to produce harmonious geometric figures.

Half-timbering: Heavy, exposed timber framework spaces filled with plaster or wattle and daub or brick. Half-timbering is used with Stick, Queen Anne, Tudor, and Jacobethan architectural styles.

Hipped roof: A roof with four equally sloped sides.

Hop: A vine grown for its papery, yellowish-green flowers, used in brewing beer. Hop flowers grow in conelike clusters. The petals have tiny glands that contain various oils and resins that prevent the growth of bacteria in beer and give the beverage its bitter taste. Washington is the leading hop-growing state, while Oregon ranks second.

Ionic order: A Grecian order composed of a fluted column with a base and a capital, usually parallel to the architrave, consisting of two pairs of spiral ornaments known as volutes.

Jerkinhead roof: A gable roof truncated or clipped at the apex.

Keystone: The wedge-shaped stone found at the center of an arch.

Le Corbusier (1887–1966): French/Swiss architect of central importance to twentieth-century architecture.

Lintel: The horizontal structural member over an opening that supports the load above it.

Loggia: A porch or open gallery that may have arches and has columns on one or both sides. Loggias are different than porches or verandas in that they are a part of the house itself and therefore more architectural.

Mansard (roof): A roof having two slopes on each of its four sides; the lower slope is much steeper than the upper slope.

Modillion: An ornamental block or bracket used in series to support the overhang in Corinthian orders.

Molding: A continuous decorative band or strip used as trim around window and door openings or in cornices. It provides a controlled transition from one surface to another.

Mullion: A vertical bar on a window or door that divides and supports the panes or panels.

Muntin: A bar of wood or metal that divides and supports panes of glass in a window.

Newel: The post at the top or bottom of a stairway, supporting the handrail.

Ogee: A pointed arch with double-curved sides, one concave, the other convex. It was widely used in decorated and perpendicular Gothic architecture.

Old Colony: In the 1950s, Eric Ladd became involved in an extensive project saving and placing together some of Portland's finer buildings. These older buildings were becoming endangered as Portland began to expand its boundaries. The project hoped to move these buildings to one area called the "Old Colony," where they would be safe from demolition. The Joseph Kamm House was one of these buildings.

Orders: In classical architecture, an order consists of a column or a pillar (with or without a base), its capital (or head), and the horizontal entablature above, which the column supports. These elements are proportioned and decorated in different styles. The three basic orders were established by the Greeks: the Doric, the Ionic, and the Corinthian. The Romans later modified these orders and added three of their own: the Tuscan, the Roman Doric, and the Composite.

Apart from the orders of the Greek Reviva style — in which an effort was made to reproduce the orders associated with the newly rediscovered architecture of ancient Greece — most of the "classical" details found in nineteenth-century houses tend to be borrowed from the Renaissance styles, which were based on the architecture of ancient Rome. Therefore, columns that closely resemble the Roman orders and Roman arches are most likely to appear on such houses.

Oriel window: A bay window supported by brackets or corbels and usually located on an upper story.

Palazzo: An Italian palace, or any large, extravagant building of a similar style.

Palladian window: Also called a Venetian window; a window in three parts: a large, arched central window flanked by two smaller rectangular windows.

Parapet: A low wall placed for protection where there is a sudden drop, such as on a rooftop or the edges of a bridge.

Pattern book: Books written and illustrated by architects that included plans, elevations, and instructions on how to build homes in popular architectural styles.

Pediment: A triangular section used as a crowning element over doors.

Picturesque: An English architectural style characterized by eclecticism, asymmetry, and a variety of texture and materials.

Pier: A column or upright thickened section of a wall that supports a building when placed at regular intervals and used like posts.

Pilaster: A rectangular column or shallow pier projecting from a wall.

Pinnacle: The highest point on a building, usually an ornamental shaft tapering to a point; found in Gothic and Gothic Revival architecture.

Pitch: The degree of slope of a roof or of a flight of stairs, windows, entryways, and so on.

Plinth: A projecting base of a wall, the square base of a pedestal, or the lower, squared part of the base of a column.

Portico: A large, roofed porch or walkway with a pedimented roof supported by columns.

Post and lintel (post and beam): A structural sytem of uprights supporting horizontal beams that span the space between them.

Pugin, A. W. N. (1812–52): He was a key influence on the development of the Gothic Revival style through the fervent rhetoric of his writings, which emphasized rationalism and moral values in design. He was a prolific designer of churches and their contents.

∽

Quoin: The cornerstone of a building that rises the entire height of the wall.

∽

Raze: To tear down; destroy completely; demolish.

Renaissance: A style that developed in Italy in the fifteenth century and spread throughout Europe. It represented a return to Roman standards and motifs, but it developed regional variations in France, Germany, and Britain.

Richardson, Henry Hobson (1838–86): He studied architecture in Europe and America and became inspired by Romanesque architecture, which was characterized by monumental masonry forms and round-arched openings.

Rococo: An early eighteenth-century style, mainly French, characterized by lightness of color and form and an excess of decoration.

Romanesque: The style of art and architecture preceding Gothic, prevalent in Europe during the eleventh and twelfth centuries. It is characterized by the use of massive masonry and thick proportions, round arches, and vaulting.

Ruskin, John (1819–1900): English writer and critic who had an immense influence on both the Gothic Revival and the Arts and Crafts movements.

Rustication: A type of masonry in which stone blocks are separated by deeply grooved joints. The masonry may be smooth or roughly textured.

∽

Sash: A window framework that is fixed or movable. It has movable slides or fixed pivots.

Segmental arch: An arch formed by an arc or segment of a circle.

Shingles: Wooden tiles used for covering roofs and walls.

Shiplag siding: Wooden siding grooved along the horizontal plane so that the boards join as a tongue and groove.

Siding: The narrow horizontal or vertical wooden boards that form the outer face of the walls in a traditional wood-frame house. More loosely, the term describes any material that can be applied to the outside of a building as a finish.

Spindle: A short, decorative-turned piece, such as a baluster or newel, often used in and around porch openings and sometimes forming an entablature.

Stick work: The decorative, stick-like pieces of wood placed in diagonal, vertical, and horizontal patterns on the outside of a wood-frame building.

Stucco: An exterior wall covering consisting of a mixture of cement, sand, lime, and water or of cement, sand, and hair.

Sunbursts: An Eastlake decorative element shaped like a sun with radiating rays.

Swag: A decoration resembling a garland of fruit, flower, or leaves draped between two points.

∽

Terra cotta: A kind of material made of a fine grade of clay and fired at a high temperature. Generally it was manufactured in hollow blocks, 4 inches deep, with faces typically 12 x 18 inches.

Tongue and groove: A joint made by fitting a projecting strip along the edge of one board into a groove cut along the edge of another board.

Transom: A small rectangular window above a door or other window.

Trim molding: A continuous decorative band that can be employed on both the interior or exterior of a building.

Tudor arch: A four-centered pointed arch, characteristic of Tudor-style architecture in England in the fifteenth and sixteenth centuries.

Turret: A small tower.

Tuscan order: A Roman order. Its decoration is distinguished by its nonfluted, unadorned columns. It is very simple and strong.

Tympanum: The area above the lintel of a doorway and below the arch above it; the space enclosed by the moldings of a pediment.

∽

Vault: An arched roof or ceiling of brick, stone, or concrete.

Veranda: An open space attached to the exterior wall of a building, usually with a roof supported by columns or posts.

Vernacular: Local or regional architecture using local materials, local building techniques, and local approaches to design. Generally it is applied to architecture in preindustrial societies where there was no division of labor between designer and builder or where buildings have not been professionally designed.

Victorian architecture: A building style popular in England during the reign of Queen Victoria (1840–1901) characterized by picturesque forms inspired by medieval buildings.

Volute: A spiral, scroll-like ornament found on Ionic or Composite capitals.

∽

Water table: A ledge or molding that projects from the first floor level of a building to protect the foundation from rain water.

Wave scroll: A type of molding designed to look like connected breaking waves.

Weatherboards: Overlapping horizontal timber boards that cover a wood-framed building. Also called clapboards. In older houses, horizontal lines of the overlaps are from four to six inches apart.

Widow's walk: An observation platform, usually with a railing, built on the roof of a house; especially found on coastal houses for the purpose of overlooking the sea.

∽

Bibliography

Alderman, L. R. "The New One-Story Schoolhouse, Showing the Possibilities of Such Buildings as Developed on the Pacific Coast." *Ladies Home Journal*, April 1916. 4.

Arnheim, Rudolf. *The Dynamics of Architectural Form*. Berkeley: University of California, 1977.

Belluschi, Peitro. Forward to *Wade Hampton Pipes*, by Ann Brewster Clarke. Portland: Binford & Mort, 1986.

Bennett, Albert B., Jr., and Leonard T. Nelson. *Mathematics: An Informal Approach*. 2nd ed. Boston: Allyn & Bacon, 1985.

Bicknell, A. J. *Specimen Book of One Hundred Architectural Designs*. New York: A. J. Bicknell, 1878.

Bicknell Village Builder. *Bicknell's Victorian Buildings: Floor Plans and Elevations for 45 Houses and Other Structures*. New York: A. J. Bicknell, 1878; New York: Dover, 1979.

Borissavlievitch, Miloutine. *The Golden Number and the scientific aesthetics of architecture*. New York: Philosophical Library, 1958.

Brolin, Brent C. *Flight of Fancy: The Banishment and Return of Ornament*. New York: St. Martin's Press, 1985.

Brunelleschi, Filippo. *The Renaissance Rediscovery of Linear Perspective*. New York: Harper & Row, 1976.

Burton, David M. *The History of Mathematics: An Introduction*. 2nd ed. Iowa: Wm. C. Brown, 1988.

Carley, Rachel. *The Visual Dictionary of American Domestic Architecture*. New York: Henry Holt, 1994.

Clark, Roger H., and Michael Pause. *Precedents in Architecture*. 2nd ed. New York: Van Hostrand Reinhold, 1996.

Clark, Rosalind. *Oregon Style, Architecture from 1840 to the 1950s*. Portland: Professional Book Center, 1983.

Cleaver, J. D. *Island Immigrants: The Bybees and the Howells*. Sauvie Island Heritage Series 2, vol 2. Portland: Oregon Historical Society, 1986.

Comstock, William T. *Country Houses and Seaside Cottages of the Victorian Era*. New York: Dover, 1989.

Conway, Hazel, and Rowan Roenisch. *Understanding Architecture: An introduction to architecture and architectural history*. London & New York: Routledge, 1994.

Crane, Walter. *Line and Form*. London: Bell & Sons, 1921.

———*The Claims of Decorative Art*. Boston: Houghtin Mifflin, 1892.

———*The Bases of Design*. London: Ge. Bell, 1904.

Damaz, Paul. *Art in European Architecture*. New York: Reinhold Publishing, 1956.

D'Espouy, Hector, ed. *Greek and Roman Architecture in Classic Drawings*. New York: Dover, 1981.

Downing, Andrew Jackson. *The Architecture of Country Houses*. New York: Da Capo Press, 1968.

Dresser, Christopher. *Principles of Decorative Design*. 4th ed. London & New York: Cassell, Petter, Galpin & Co., 1873.

Eastlake, Charles. *Hints on Household Taste*. Reprint, New York: Dover, 1969.

Farey, Cyril A. *Architectural Drawing, Perspective & Rendering*. London: Batsford Limited, 1949.

Fletcher, Bannister. *A History of Architecture on the Comparative Method*. 19th ed. New York: Scribner, 1963.

Friedman, Ralph. *In Search of Western Oregon*. Caldwell, Idaho: Caxton Printers, 1990.

Gloag, John. *Victorian Taste: Some Social Aspects of Architecture and Industrial Design from 1820–1900*. New York: Macmillan, 1962.

Grabow, Stephen. *Christopher Alexander: The Search for a New Paradigm in Architecture*. Boston: Oriel, 1983.

Guptill, Arthur L. *Rendering in Pen and Ink*. Edited by Susan E. Meyer. 1976. New York: Watson-Guptill, 1997.

Hale, Jonathan. *The Old Way of Seeing*. Boston: Houghton Mifflin, 1994.

Harmon, Rick, ed. *Special Issue: Aspects of Portland History*. Vol. 99, no. 3 of *Oregon Historical Quarterly*. Portland: Oregon Historical Society, 1998.

Harrison, Henry S. *Houses: The Illustrated Guide to Construction, Design & Systems*. 3rd ed. Chicago: Real Estate Education, 1973.

Hawkins, William J., III, and William F. Willingham. *Classic Houses of Portland, Oregon 1850–1950*. Portland: Timber, 1999.

Herbst, Joyce. *Oregon Coast*. Vol. 2 of *Discovering Old Oregon Series*. Portland: Frank Amato, 1985.

Holly, Henry Hudson. *Country Seats and Modern Dwellings: Two Victorian domestic architectural stylebooks*. New York: American Life Foundation and Study Institute, 1977.

Howell, Thomas. *Flora of Northwest America*. Portland: Thomas Howell, 1903.

Keller, Paul. *Portland Vignettes*. Text by Sam Raddon. Portland: Metropolitan Press, 1935.

King, Anthony D. *The Bungalow: The Production of a Global Culture*. 2nd ed. New York: Oxford University, 1995.

King's Hill Walking Tour. Portland: Goose Hollow Foothills League, 1980.

Matson, Cecil. *The Way It Was: A Kaleidoscopic Look at Early Theater in the Oregon

Country and a View of the Changing Pattern of Theatre in the Early Years of the Twentieth Century into the Present Day. Portland: C. Matson, 1988.

Moss, Roger W., and Gail Caskey Winkler. *Victorian Exterior Decoration*. New York: Henry Holt, 1987.

Navaersen, Kenneth. *West Coast Victorians: A Nineteenth-Century Legacy*. Wilsonville, Ore: Beautiful America, 1987.

Norman, James. *Oregon Main Street: A Rephotographic Survey*. Portland: Oregon Historical Society, 1994.

———*Oregon's Architectural Heritage: The National Register Properties of the Portland Area*. Portland: Solo Press, 1986.

———*Portland's Architectural Heritage*. Portland: Oregon Historical Society, 1986.

O'Donnell, Terence. "Oregon History." In *1999–2000 Oregon Blue Book*. 330–45. Portland: Oregon Historical Society, 1999.

O'Gorman, James F. *A B C of Architecture*. Philadelphia: University of Pennsylvania, 1998.

Porphyrios, Demetri. *Classical Architecture: The Living Tradition*. New York: McGraw Hill, 1992.

Porter, Tom. *How Architects Visualize*. New York: Van Nostrand Reinhold, 1979.

Prideaux, Jan, ed. *Craftsman Collection: 170 Home Plans in the Craftsman & Bungalow Style*. Tuscon: Home Planners, 1999.

Quennell, Marjorie. *Everyday Things in Ancient Greece*. 2nd ed. New York: Putnam, 1930.

Redgrave, Richard. *Manual of Design*. New York: Schribner, Welford, & Armstrong, 1876.

Reece, Daphne. *Historic Houses of the Pacific Northwest*. San Franscisco: Chronicle Books, 1985.

Scott, Geoffrey. *Architecture of Humanism*. New York: Charles Scribner, 1969.

Society of Architectural Historians. *Buildings of the United States*. New York: Oxford University, 1993.

Speltz, Alexander. *Styles of Ornament*. New York: Grosset & Dunlap, 1936.

Stickley, Gustav, ed. *Craftsman Bungalows: 59 homes from the Craftsman. Articles came from the periodical called The Craftsman published monthly from 1901–1916*. Introduction by Alan Weissman. New York: Dover, 1988.

Viollet-le-Duc, Eugene-Emmanuel. *The Architectural Theory of Viollet-le-Duc*. Cambridge: MIT, 1990.

Vitruvius. *The Ten Books on Architecture*. Translated by Morris Hicky Morgan. Cambridge: Harvard University, 1914; New York: Dover, 1960.

Wheeler, Gervase. *Rural Homes*. N.p., 1851.

Woodward, George E., and Edward G. Thompson. *A Victorian Housebuilder's Guide*. 1869. Reprint, New York: Dover, 1988.

Index

Albany, Oregon, 14, 31
arched features, 13, 14, 19, 23, 29, 39, 41, 65, 66
Artemis, 59
Arts and Crafts style, 55, 64, 66
ashlar, 37, 64
Ashley House, 45
Augustus, 58

balustrade, 21, 23, 29, 45, 49, 53, 64
Barlow House, 25, 61
Beaux Arts style, 27, 39
brackets, 14, 21, 25, 31, 64, 65
Bungalow style, 47, 67, 68
buttress, 19, 64
Bybee House, 17, 66

casement features, 14, 47, 51, 55, 64
Classical style, 17, 29, 33, 39, 45, 53, 63, 64, 65, 67
Columbia River Railroad, 47
Corinthian columns, 45, 53, 58, 63, 64
cornice, 17, 23, 25, 29, 49, 53, 59, 64, 65
Craftsman Magazine, 47, 55, 68

Donation Land Claim Act of 1850, 17, 25, 31, 64
Doric features, 45, 58, 59, 64, 65
Downing, Andrew Jackson, 19, 21, 67

Eastlake style, 31, 35, 37, 66, 67
English influence, 45, 47, 51, 53, 55, 56, 65, 66

Flemish influence, 29
Flippin House, 33
Flora of Northwest America, 17, 67
French style, 13, 23, 33, 39, 65, 66

gable, 17, 27, 29, 31, 33, 35, 37, 45, 49, 54, 64, 65
Georgian style, 45
Glisan Building, 23
golden proportions, 13, 17, 60, 65, 67
Gothic style, 14, 15, 19, 25, 27, 65, 66

Heusner House, 37
hipped roof, 21, 25, 31, 37, 41, 65
Hochstedler House, 31

Holford, William G., 51
Hollywood Theatre, 43, 61
Honeyman-Wood House, 53, 61
hops, 51
Howe, Frank Maynard, 27
Howells, 17, 67

Ionic columns, 45, 58, 59, 64, 65, 66
Italian influences, 21, 23, 25, 29, 39, 41, 64, 65
Italianate style, 23, 25, 29

Jackson C. S., 39
Jackson Tower, 39
Journal Building, 39

Kamm House, 23, 61, 65
Kennedy Elementary School, 41, 61
King's Addition, 29
Krumbein, Justus, 23

Ladd, Eric, 23, 65
Lawrence, Ellis, 51
Lazarus, Edgar Max, 37
Lewis and Clark Expedition, 23, 37, 39
Lewis and Clark Trail, 47
Lewis, David C., 53
Livesley House, 51
Loeb, Nathan, 29

mansard roof, 23, 65
Maritime Colonial style, 49
McKim, Mead, and White architectural firm, 27
Mediterranean style, 13, 39, 41, 64
Miller House, 23
Moyer House, 21
Multnomah Conservatory of Music, 35
Multnomah County, 17, 55

Naramore, Floyd A., 41
Naval Corps, 49

Old Colony (Eric Ladd's project), 23, 65
Old Scotch Church, 19, 29
Oregon Film & Video Foundation, 43
Oregon Historical Society, 17, 67, 68
Oregon Journal, 39

Palmer House, 35
pattern book, 19, 21, 23, 29, 65
Pence, Lafayette, 45
picturesque, 19, 29, 37, 65, 66
Pipes family, Pipes House, 55
Portland School District, 41
Prohibition Reform, 53

Queen Anne style, 29, 31, 35, 37, 47, 65

Reid Brothers architectural firm, 39
Renaissance styles, 33, 39, 53, 64, 65, 66, 67
Richardsonian style, 27, 66
Richardsonian Romanesque, 27
Roman influences, 13, 27, 39, 45, 49, 53, 55, 58, 59, 64, 65, 66
Romanticism, 37
Roosevelt, Eleanore and Theodore, 49, 53, 61

sash windows, 29, 37, 45, 66
Sauvie Island, Oregon, 17
Scottish influences, 19
Seaside, Oregon, 47, 66
Seaside Promenade, 47
Second Empire, 21, 23
Senior Center in Clatskanie, 33
Shaw, Richard Norman, 29
Shingle style, 23, 33, 37, 47, 66
Southern Immigrant Route, 33
Spanish Baroque style, 43, 47
Spanish inifluences, 43, 47
Stick style, 31, 37, 64, 66
Stickley, Gustav, 47, 68
St. Mary's Chapel, 23

terra cotta, 39, 41, 66
theater in Portland, 41, 66
Therkelsen, L., 23
Tillamook Bay Coast Guard Station, 49
transom, 21, 23, 25, 29, 66
Tualatin Plains Presbyterian Church, 19
Tudor style, 29, 51, 65, 66
Tuscan columns, 17, 33, 41, 45, 49, 65, 66
tympanum, 29, 66

Union Station, 27

Van Brunt, Henry, 27
veranda, 21, 27, 37, 65, 66
Victorian influences, 13, 25, 29, 35, 66, 67, 68
Villard, Henry, 27
Vitruvius, 49, 58, 68

wedding cake design, 39
Westover Project/Terraces, 45
Wheeler, Gervais, 31
widow's walk, 45, 68
Wood, Nan, 53
World War II, 39, 49